ANGEL
WITHIN

The Art Of Mindfulness

And Slaying Demons

Audie Ward

NEWMAN SPRINGS PUBLISHING
320 Broad Street
Red Bank, NJ 07701

First originally published by Newman Springs Publishing 2022

ISBN 978-1-68498-090-1 (Paperback)
ISBN 978-1-68498-091-8 (Digital)

Printed in the United States of America

Newton's third law states that, for every action (force) in nature, there is an equal and opposite reaction. If object A exerts force on object B, object B also exerts an equal and opposite force on object A. In other words, forces result from interactions. Our thoughts become forces in our minds. How we interact with our own thoughts is very important. *Everyone* has spontaneous negative, irrational, or anxiety-laced thoughts—everyone. They are often called what-if thoughts. What's the difference between the inpatient eating eggs with his own shoelaces for utensils and him or her living a happy, fulfilled life? Don't turn a shoji thought into a limestone arena like the Roman Colosseum. A shoji is a traditional Japanese wall, doorway, or window made out of paper. It is often painted with colorful designs or slatted to hide its transparency. It looks like a real barrier to the other side, but in actuality, it is just a paper facade. Anxiety, what-if thoughts, is just shojis. Don't give irrational thoughts the force of an immovable giant object. Just walk through that shit! A positive thought can take us to the moon, or a negative thought could drag us to hell. It is up to you to determine how much force you allow a thought to have—for good or for bad. Our thoughts determine our actions, peace of mind, and quality of life. For me, this is the beginning of mindfulness.

In the spiritual war for humanity's fate, we pray that Newton was not correct. We pray that heaven's forces are not only equal to but are greater than the forces of evil. We pray that God's light is brighter than the devil's darkness.

Many religions accept that the archangel Michael led an army of angels against Lucifer and his evil companions long before Christ redeemed humanity and made open the gates of heaven for mankind. Lucifer's motivations aside, moving forward, humanity's concern is that he swore to corrupt God's greatest creation and take the earth for himself. He's still trying.

In his attack upon heaven, the devil had two hundred angels by his side, who also bet on the losing team. They were also sent to the depths of Abaddon, vowing revenge. So the game begins. They work in whispers, shadows, and nudges to corrupt righteous humans into morally flawed behaviors. (Where is the fun in corrupting the already corrupted?) They rejoice in tempting good people to do bad things. In theological text, they are known as the watchers. But they do more than just watch. This is why Newton's third law is important to humans. For every soul they corrupt and damn to being residents of Hades upon completing their contract here on earth, the more powerful Lucifer becomes. So as Lucifer exerts force upon humans and earth, God must also meet that force with more intent so that the balance of good and evil is tipped in his favor.

Humans are not as easily influenced as you might think. Remember that God made us in his image. That image is not weak. The devil takes advantage of people in weakened conditions. Drugs, alcohol, and anything that softens the mind makes way for the person to be influenced. Take for example a watcher loitering about a bar waiting for someone to get drunk enough that he or she feels disembodied.

The watcher whispers in this person's ear, "It's okay to drive. I can make it home."

Clearly the person is hammered and shouldn't drive, but that little voice inside his or her head says, 'I can make it.' Any carnage or destruction that ensues is a win for the watcher. This is a small win for a watcher. The ultimate prize is a step-in or a walk-in. They temporarily take control of the disembodied human, and that's when really bad shit happens.

Imagine this: A man and a woman are drunk at a crowded bar. Under normal circumstances, neither would have a sexual one-night stand with the other. But with their inhibitions removed, they are susceptible to influence. The watcher whispers in their ears. Before they know it, they rationalize the behavior, and they are at his or her place having sex. This is part of the watcher's plan. The man and woman are dysphoric, disembodied, and like an open door to your house when you are not home—anyone can just walk in. The watcher inhabits the man temporarily. He feels all of the human senses, the warmth of human touch. He sees through his human host's eyes and, for a moment, inhabits God's greatest creation. If a pregnancy results from the encounter, the baby is not a full Nephilim (spawn of watchers and mortal women), but the baby has been marked. Throughout this person's life, man or woman, he or she could be walked in without the protection of God's grace. A watcher would not have to weaken their body or mind to exert influence. This practice of seed planting is not done and is forbidden to angels. You might ask, Where is the equal and opposite reaction from our angels? Remember, Jesus was tempted by the devil for forty days and forty nights without giving in. Humans have free will. But if we weaken our souls and open pathways to be corrupted, then we have the challenge of resistance.

This does not mean that God leaves us to our own free will and doesn't step in and help. We are important to him. God has bestowed divine gifts upon us and assigned angels to aid us in our fight. Joshua, the successor of Moses, was a warrior for God for forty years. He knew only friend or foe. One day, an angel appeared to him on a hill on the eve of battle.

Joshua charged at him with sword drawn and commanded the man to answer, "Are you friend or foe?"

The angel replied, "I am neither."

Joshua was extraordinary in battle. His gifts were legendary. He knew only war for his entire life, but in this event, he knew the war was over. Indeed, he was touched by God. Throughout time, God's emissaries have given some humans divine gifts. The divine gift of prophecy is one of the most powerful and rare of these gifts. The archangel Gabriel is most often tasked with choosing the recipient of such a gift. But the rules of engagement are different for angels than that of demons. Angels can't walk in or influence like dark forces because of the whole freewill shit. Angels are usually working through signs or dreams (if the person has the gift to receive a message in a dream). On occasion, a child is born, who is the descendant of someone great, who was touched by God, like Joshua. If this child should befall a tragedy like early death, an angel is allowed to do more than just give vague signs that might not be seen or to give a dream that might be remembered. This is when an angel can become incarnate and make a difference in the war. Life is not easy for either, which brings us to this story.

Buffalo, New York, August 9, 1969. A child is born to Mark and Helen D'Antoni. Lucas Santino D'Antoni came into this world with a fate and destiny that were not of his making. Like a beacon on a dark night, his birth was noticed. Heaven and hell saw the light. Lucas was a descendant of the prophet Moses. Lucas had an older brother, Michael, from his mother's previous marriage. He had two sisters from Mark and Helen—Marcy, who was six years older, and a younger sister, Yvette, who would come a couple of years later. Lucas's grandfather was born in Italy and migrated to the United States before WWII. He got his citizenship by joining the army and was a paratrooper. On D-Day, he was in a hang glider and landed on Utah Beach. All in all, he made about sixteen jumps behind enemy lines during the war. He had unnaturally good luck. He met Lucas's grandmother in England, where they eventually had Lucas's father. Yes, his grandfather was also a descendant of Moses; but just after the war, he fell off a ladder while cleaning the drains on his house and developed a traumatic brain injury. His spiritual potential and usefulness to God were never realized. Lucas's father's potential also cut short the watchers. This time, they used addiction to snuff out any attempts by God to utilize the lineage of Moses.

In the fall of 1974, the watchers took no chances with the lineage of Moses this time. Lucas was five years old; and his older brother, Michael, was seven. They shared the same room and had to sleep in the same bed. At about 3:00 a.m., Michael awoke to the bed shaking uncontrollably like an earthquake, except nothing else was shaking. Michael looked over at Lucas and saw that he started to convulse violently. The irony was that the bed shaking precipitated Lucas's event. Michael ran into his parents' bedroom. He was frantic and yelled that Lucas wasn't breathing. His mother ran into the kids' room overcome by terror. Even his sedated father responded in disbelief of what Michael was reporting. It was worse than Michael thought; when they got to Lucas's room, he was not breathing and had no pulse. Marcy called for an ambulance, and everyone did what they could. But it appeared that Lucas was dead, and the watchers had diminished the light of Moses again. Or so they thought.

The archangel Michael was witness to this and froze time. It was a momentous thundering boom from the heavens that shook the earth. But not even the celebrating watchers were aware of Michael's intervention. Michael, the most powerful angel, summoned Gabriel, the messenger, and Raguel of justice to the baby's room. Gabriel was a huge, foreboding figure. The mere sight of him invoked fear. His appearance reflected a lifetime of battles, but his heart and aura were pure peace with a golden light. Raguel was not as intimidating as Gabriel, but he was no slouch either. He emanated a purplish light but was definitely confident with the posture of pride. This was not a two-way conversation. This was to give marching orders. For a moment, there was silence as the three angels surveyed the scene. Michael was all business.

But then Gabriel turned to Raguel and said, "Hey, Rags," (a nickname he had).

Michael announced that the circumvention of the line of Moses stopped now. Michael knew that, if he or the other archangels were to go missing from heaven, it would be seen by the forces of darkness. But Raguel, a just and wise angel (but not so publicly known), would not be seen as missing. Michael cannot stop time for a long period, so he kept his commands brief. He instructed Raguel to become incarnate with Lucas and protect him. Think of it as two people in a car, but only one gets to drive at a time. He strictly told Raguel not to reveal his consciousness to Lucas, but his direction would be made clear. Michael then told Gabriel to communicate with Lucas in dreams, whispers, and nudges but to be subtle. With brief instruction and the baby Lucas frozen and unresponsive, Raguel's figure began to become translucent, and his purplish aura transformed into an orblike shape. As Raguel entered Lucas's lifeless body and his mother was frozen in a position of chest compressions of CPR, Michael and Gabriel disappeared, and baby Lucas opened his eyes and began to cough.

There were two watchers in the room, Azazel and Lilith. Azazel was ancient and had been corrupting mankind since the fall of Lucifer. He was calculating and intelligent. He was evil, pure evil, and diabolical. Lilith was impetuous, evil with a temper that knew no limits. She had a seductive, tempting appearance but was pale and gaunt. Neither was very pleased to see life breathed back into Lucas, but Azazel held it in. Lilith was enraged and began to reach into Lucas's heart to squeeze it and kill him once more. Azazel called to her to stop instinctually, but she continued. They were not flesh but more temporal, so she reached through Lucas's chest. She was expelled from him violently and lost awareness for a brief moment. They looked at each other with bewilderment and then vanished.

In the days that followed, Lucas's mother had him in the hospital for testing daily without fail. His head was shaved for brain scans. He was in primitive MRI tubes for scanning. He had several EKGs. Nothing was discovered to be wrong with him. By all accounts, he was a normal five-year-old. The doctors hypothesized that it may have been an anomalous seizure and recommended preventative medication. Lucas suffered through seizure meds until he was twelve years old. He was sedated basically, lethargic, and not developing physically. His older sister, Marcy, pleaded with their mother to get him off the meds. She felt sorry for him, almost like he was drunk and stumbling through childhood. Lucas was always with his mother. Everywhere she went, she took him with her. The medication wasn't his only challenge.

The first thing the watchers did to fuck with Lucas was conscious paralysis. His mind would be awake, but he was catatonic. At first, it was funny for them to watch the family dog lick his face while he lay there unable to move. Then they started with visiting him in his dreams. In one dream, he entered an elevator. It mirrored inside.

As he entered and turned around to face the door, he saw his reflection. He saw that he was about fifteen years old, but that did not alarm him even though he was actually about six at this time. There were two men behind him that were about midthirties, clean-cut Caucasian men with dark hair slicked back dressed in 1970s suits. The man on his right moved a little and drew Lucas's attention. The man calmly opened his mouth to smile and revealed vampirelike fangs. Lucas awoke in a panic, terrified. In a series of dreams, Lucas was chased by grotesque monsters. Lucas would create small wormholes in the dreams to run from the monsters in an attempt to escape. Remember, this was the early 1970s. Things like this weren't on TV. There were no superhero movies where images like this could seep into a child's subconscious. This was not something a five—to twelve-year-old should have to face, but the watchers were relentless in their attempts to cripple Lucas with fear. Lucas would lie in bed afraid to sleep for fear of the battle he would face, so much so that even closing his eyes would reveal the faces of demons.

But Raguel was ordered not to influence him. These were battles that were necessary for Lucas to fight and overcome to prepare him for what he would face in the future. Gabriel placed items in his path to assist Lucas in his challenges. After all, Michael did tell him to help with whispers and nudges. Lucas read a comic book where a human could transform his body completely into metal. Lucas thought that, if he could do that in his dreams, no fanged bastard could hurt him. This time, he wasn't sleeping at all. When everyone went to bed, he would wander the streets of Buffalo, climbing telephone poles and sliding down on the cables. He was about ten years old when he had had enough. In his next demonic dream, he was going g to be Colossus!

Like before, he entered the elevator. There were two men behind him. The man smiled again, revealing his fangs, but was interrupted by a metal hand around his throat. Lucas was about seven feet tall and made of metal after screaming, "Colossus!"

Lucas told the vampire, "I'm no fun to play with anymore."

Until now, Raguel and Gabriel hadn't really influenced or nudged Lucas too much. These early battles were his own.

Lucas would often pray to God, asking, "What are you preparing me for?"

Lucas grew up Catholic and believed. Every night before sleeping, he would say the Our Father, Hail Mary, the Apostles' Creed, and the Act of Contrition. Then he would make requests for the protection of his family— Yvette, Marcy, Michael, and his mother, sometimes his father.

In the fall of 1979, when Lucas was about ten years old, his grandfather passed away. The war hero who had survived WWII had succumbed to a heart attack while unloading a moving truck, his final years spent struggling with his traumatic brain injury after falling from the ladder. Lucas had a dream on the morning of his grandfather's funeral. His grandfather appeared to Lucas in the kitchen of the house that Lucas lived in. Lucas could hear his grandfather's voice although his mouth was not moving. His grandfather appeared as an old man as he was at the time of his death. But then he began to get younger as he spoke until he was a healthy, fit young man wearing his military uniform. His grandfather told Lucas that he was okay and in a better place. He told Lucas he would be with him and look after Lucas throughout his life. His grandfather only appeared to Lucas before ascending to heaven. The archangel Uriel showed him the way as he had done for centuries, as was his mandate by God.

Lucas would remember the song playing on the radio on the way to his grandfather's burial for the rest of his life—"American Pie" by Don Mclean. While the song may have been about famous artists like Elvis, the Beatles, or Tom Petty, Lucas never liked the lyric "The Father, Son, and Holy Ghost caught the last train for the coast." Lucas always felt that God would never abandon mankind even if music disappeared. Hey, it's the logic of a ten-year-old, even a special ten-year-old who had already been through a lot. This event also clued Lucas into the fact that he was different. What did this dream indicate? Did Grandpa visit anyone else after he passed? Did anyone else see him? He told his parents and sisters about the dream. He even told his grandmother about the dream (his father's mother). No one had any similar experience. He was beginning to sense the presence of Raguel, or perhaps he had a spiritual doorway that was opened in him that was not in others. While this was happening, it was time for Raguel to learn of Archangel Michael's plans for Lucas. Michael appeared to Raguel in the deep reaches of Lucas's mind. They spoke of their pride in the way Lucas was developing and his limitless spiritual potential. Michael told Raguel to be his inner voice disguised as instinct or intuition but to avoid exposing his consciousness to Lucas. He said that Lucas would be of service to the world but to hide his true nature from the forces of darkness for as long as possible. This is the extent of God's plan that he needed to know.

Lucas was kind of born forty years old. When he turned twelve, his parents decided that he had gone seven years without a seizure and it was time to take him off medication. His world changed. He began to grow. Raguel and Gabriel could reach him in dreams now. The training began, mostly the ability to fly and think in his dreams. You see, Lucas had the ability not to just be a spectator in his dreams; he could affect the outcomes. At first, he didn't want to fly too high or too far because he was afraid he would fall or not make it back to his body. But he had learned from his early watcher dreams that he would be okay. The dark dreams stopped and positive, really positive, spiritual dreams began. He could sleep now and grow.

Although his spiritual life was getting better, real life was not. He lived in a very poor part of Buffalo. His father worked in air-conditioning when he worked but was so sedated with tranquilizers that he rarely spoke to Lucas. His father was also a part-time guitarist and played a gig here and there for little money. But he dragged Lucas around shitty bars and rooms for offtrack betting where reptilian energy filled the rooms. Lucas was allergic to cigarette smoke by the time he was ten. His father would pretend to go to work after quitting a job and drag Lucas to rich neighborhoods to sell "I Love NY" buttons for a fake cause just to acquire enough money for cigarettes. Needless to say, government cheese and food stamps weren't strangers to Lucas.

His mother worked three jobs just to pay the bills. Thankfully Lucas could talk to his mother. She knew about his struggles and his dreams. Rather than taking him to a shrink, she took him to their local priest. Father Tim was cool. He rode a Harley and wore a leather jacket. Father Tim was trepidatious but believed that there was something special about Lucas. He told Lucas something that would shape his life, at least for a while.

He said, "Don't shine. If you shine, you will attract attention. Put it away and forget it's part of you."

Lucas did just that, even going so far as to announce that he was going to go by his middle name from now on. From then on, he was Santino, but his friends could call him Sonny.

Sonny excelled in creativity. While his sisters were more linear and mathematical, he was creative. He was a problem solver and a communicator and funny and quick witted. His unfortunate experiences of scamming people out of their money selling buttons for smokes did equip him with a talent for being difficult to argue with.

He was still small and skinny and the very opposite of tough but smarter than would-be thugs that would try to intimidate him. His father, for all his faults, did assist with his mental strengthening. Mark taught Sonny how to play chess. And, boy, could he play chess. He was beating his father by the age of ten. He saw that his father relied too much on his knights, and if one or both were taken away, his pop was toast. Sonny would trade randomly with pieces just to take a knight from his father. Once he did that, it was over. Just like the watchers in his early dreams, he was no fun to play with anymore. He did what Father Tim advised. He put the shine away and was just another poor kid in the projects. But how long would that last? High school was next, but he was too scrawny to attend public school. His growth was stunted, and his mother was concerned that he would get beat up badly and often. She arranged for him to get tested for admission into an elite technical school upstate. Based on his street savvy and artistic skills, she thought he had a shot. His IQ came back at 161, which is apparently not too shabby.

He got in. He took the city bus to school and then home again to his neighborhood. His first year at Madison Tech was great. He got to use tools and instruments for graphic design that he didn't know existed. He was doing well, and his instructors saw his potential. His mother was happy, and life settled into almost normalcy. But wait; there's more.

Sonny is Italian and lived in an Italian hood. He took a job working at a deli making sandwiches and stocking shelves for pocket cash. It was owned by two wannabe gangsters named Jimmy and Johnny Assholio! It was fine at first. He sliced deli meat, made sausages, and flirted with neighborhood girls. By this time, Sonny's father had left for the West Coast, abandoning his kids and his wife. In the mid-'80s, many large businesses were leaving Buffalo and leaving thousands without jobs. His father said he was going to Alaska to work on the pipeline, but he was actually going to Los Angeles for another woman. Sonny, his mom, and younger sister, Yvette, survived and life moved on. Sonny's siblings had their own lives to live and weren't around much. About halfway through what would be his junior year of high school, he was slicing meat at the deli, and it was too small for the protective guard. Sonny cut the tip of his right index finger off. Oops!

Jimmy Assholio put Sonny in his Porsche 911 Turbo and started to the nearest ER because all deli owners have a car like that. Jimmy told Sonny that he was going to have to tell the hospital that he was his nephew because he couldn't afford a workers' comp hustle or have his business closed down. Sonny complied and got stitched up. No calls to Mom. No help from angels.

When they got back to the deli, Jimmy was bragging to his brother, Johnny, about how Sonny didn't snitch. His reward, two twenty-something-age prostitutes. Azazel and Lilith appeared to attempt their typical whispering. Sonny was fifteen years old. The evil in the room was palpable. The watchers whispered in Sonny's ears, but Sonny wouldn't have it. Sonny refused the prostitutes, told the wannabe gangsters that it had been a long day, and excused himself. Jimmy and Johnny didn't need assistance from watchers to be assholes.

Johnny called Sonny a faggot and asked rhetorically, "What's the matter with you? You could have had both of those chicks sucking your dick in the cooler!"

Johnny said aloud that Sonny would talk and they should just kill him now because they had to send money up the chain and couldn't afford problems with their business. It was insinuated that the business was a front for the mafia, and they had responsibilities. Jimmy told Sonny it was okay and he could go. Scare tactic or the real deal, it worked. Sonny was rattled. He went home and told his mother what happened. What mom wants to hear that shit? Hadn't Sonny put her through enough? But she was calm and kinda street smart herself. Helen told Sonny that he was going to go back to the deli tomorrow. He was to tell the Assholio brothers thank you for the opportunity, but he was going to concentrate on school.

When he got to the deli the next day, Jimmy was the only one there. Sonny did as he was instructed, and Jimmy was okay with it, telling Sonny he could stock the coolers for extra cash whenever he wanted. Sonny shook Jimmy's hand and left. Sonny never saw them again.

Until now, Raguel had mostly been dormant, only assisting here and there but allowing Sonny to fight his own battles and develop his spiritual strength. But the brighter the light, the more attention it brought. Sonny's emotional courage was not invisible. Azazel and Lilith knew that they had successfully killed Lucas/Sonny when he was five but still hadn't caught on that Archangel Michael had saved him by Raguel's incarnation. They hadn't attempted to terrify him in dreams in two to three years, which allowed Archangel Gabriel and Raguel time to strengthen his spiritual gifts, particularly the divine gift of prophecy, which was in his bloodline thanks to Moses. The dreams started with seemingly minor important things. For example, a vision of what was being served in the cafeteria that day at school, and then the exact event in reality would occur. It's just like lifting weights; you start out with lighter weights and then work your way up. Between fifteen to sixteen years old, Sonny put some work in. But many of the dreams would go unnoticed, so Gabriel and Raguel would vary the times to see where Sonny responded to the best. They would give him a dream at about 3:00 a.m. and then try to go pop him up so he'd remember. If that didn't work, they would wake him up at about 6:00 a.m., let him go back to sleep, and then give him a prophecy. This was the ticket. Prophecies or out-of-body dreams were almost daily. Sometimes the dreams were not prophetic but positively charged dreams of spiritual enlightenment to upgrade his system.

For example, Sonny found himself in a supercharged flow of rushing water like a river. There was absolutely no fear, just an amazing, peaceful bliss. There were all manners of animals with him traveling to the same place with no ill intent toward each other, just all flowing to the same place. There were tigers, elephants, zebra, alligators, etc.—animals that would never get along in life but were all sharing the same supercharged positive energy. It was like Noah's ark without the ark. Sonny awoke with a feeling that he had just gotten a glimpse of heaven. The dream was short though. Sonny wanted to go back. The fact is that angels can't show a glimpse of heaven for too long, or it will get noticed. Think of it like when the police are trying to trace a call. If the call is too short, it's hard to trace, but the location will be discovered if the call goes long enough. Sonny had other positive outlets. He was too small for football or basketball, but he did practice tae kwon do. A fantastic Korean immigrant called Master Rhe. At Sonny's size, learning tae kwon do didn't make him a threat to just about anyone, but it was good for his soul and his ability to sleep. He only had a couple of friends—Jin from tae kwon do and Joseppi from the neighborhood.

About halfway through his junior year of high school, his father called. He told Sonny's mom he wasn't in Alaska working on the pipeline. He was living in Los Angeles, and he wanted her to come out there and bring Sonny and Yvette. Helen, being a good Catholic woman, sought advice from Father Tim. He told her that a woman's place is with her husband and she should go. Sonny wasn't thrilled with the idea. He was almost a black belt, and he and Jin and Jin's family had grown close. Sonny had taken second place to Jin in the New York junior Olympics in tae kwon do. (Sonny could have won the contest, but he couldn't fight his hardest versus a friend) The deciding factor, Jimmy and Johnny Assholio. Not too long ago, he was in a room with them, and they had threatened to kill him. That threat was probably past, but Sonny could sense that the situation was not over. This was one of Sonny's first nudges while conscious. In the past, Gabriel and Raguel had communicated with him in dreams and signs, but now he was upgraded and ready for a higher level of communication—nudges. Some call it intuition or a sixth sense. Yeah, like that with an exclamation point. Sonny, Yvette, and Helen talked and decided that they would move to Los Angeles to be with their father. It would be some time until they would see Marcy or Michael again. Michelle went into the army, and Marcy had a newborn son of her own.

Next stop—LA.

Sonny was enrolled in a public school in LA. It was very different from Madison Tech, where he was left alone to develop his graphic design art skills. He was a small Italian kid with a leather jacket, curly hair, and an accent. Art class was studying the graffiti on the walls and trying to interpret what gang wanted to kill which gang. He was bullied a bit but was slick and had great survivor skills. Azazel and Lilith would take turns whispering in low-vibrational bullies' ears to pick on Sonny. Einstein theorized that all energy was merely matter condensed to vibrational atoms. Lower/slower vibrating atoms were an indicator of lower intelligence (higher-vibrational people were conversely more intelligent).

Most of the time, Sonny's angels did not interfere with his free will. They would allow him to make mistakes and learn from them as long as the mistake did not lead to catastrophe. He made friends with two twins who took karate at a YMCA, and they developed a friendship. Ivory and Steven were superior physically—both six feet, two inches, with not an ounce of fat or fear and basically fully developed grown men for being sixteen years of age. They were good kids with similar father figures. Two Black kids from LA with a shitty father had a lot in common with an Italian kid from New York with a shitty father. Around a week before Christmas in about 1988, Sonny came home from school to find a note from his father on the table.

It was next to some government cheese and $40. He was gone again, gone to play guitar in a shitty band in some shitty town with some shitty woman. Sonny's mother worked three jobs to keep food on the table, but that meant that she wasn't around much. Sonny and Yvette were basically raising themselves even though they didn't hang out much. They had separate lives with different friends. Yvette assimilated to living on the West Coast better than Sonny. She was a couple of years younger and pretty, so she made friends easier. Michael was still in the military, and Marcy was living a couple of hours away in Fresno. This was not the time for Raguel to push too much for Sonny to use his spiritual gifts because surviving teenage years in LA from NY was enough. Sonny got his black belt in karate and grew taller. He was about five feet, nine inches, when he graduated from high school.

Now what?

Police departments used to have a program for kids that were between eighteen to twenty where they could take reports and work around the station until they were twenty-one and could test to be a police officer, a natural calling for Sonny to be of service. He was free from the burdens of fitting in at high school and focused on a career. He tested for the position along with six hundred other kids and tested in the top two. About three months after graduating from high school, he was a police cadet. Rome wasn't built in a day, and neither was the spiritual warrior that Sonny was destined to become. But Archangel Michael had a plan. Rags was dormant for the most part, but now Sonny was nineteen. Sonny began to grow physically. The antiseizure meds he was on until he was twelve stunted his growth, but by the time he was twenty, he was six feet, two inches. Imagine a young police officer walking around with a gun still growing. The pain in his tibias and fibulas was excruciating. He grew fast and gained muscle fast. By the time he was twenty-four, he weighed 210 pounds and had about 6 percent body fat, just like Ivory and Steven. The once meek and small kid that told two wannabe gangsters no thanks in the face of them threatening his life was just as strong physically as he was mentally. It was crazy to him. To think that he was that size. Sonny appreciated what he had been through and had an affinity for the underdog. He would become a sheepdog for the flock and a protector of the innocent.

Sonny bought his first house when he was twenty-four years old. He wasn't some awkward skinny kid anymore. He was a handsome young man with a police career and the world ahead of him. After a graveyard shift one morning, he and some other officers went to a bar after work. Strange to be drinking a beer at eight o'clock in the morning, but that's what graveyard cops do. Sonny's friends were stepping on top of each other to attract the bartender's attention. Her name was Christine, and she was beautiful. She was a little older than Sonny, with long, curly dark hair and dark skin. Sonny was quiet and didn't exactly see himself the way he looked to the world. Sonny and Christine struck up a conversation amidst the others making fools of themselves, and he asked her out. Christine was older and sexy, but she had some demons of her own that she was dealing with. They dated for about six months, and it was a good education for Sonny.

The best thing that came out of the relationship was Dino. Dino was a wolf-hybrid pup that the two picked out together in Sacramento. Sonny loved dogs. The couple did some research and found a wolf-hybrid breeder in Sac and traveled to look at a litter. This particular breeder mixed the Mackenzie wolf with Siberian huskies. The result was a huge wolf dog with mostly the temperament of a husky. Dino was silver, gray, and white and grew to be about 165 pounds.

When they picked him out from the litter of pups, Sonny asked the breeder, "Which one eats first?"

Sonny wanted the alpha male of the litter, which also meant that he would have his hands full. Sonny and Dino had a special bond that he would come to realize later in life that he would not have with another dog. He would have many but none like Dino. The relationship with Christine crashed and burned, but at least he got a great dog out of it. Dino kept him company through a time in his life when he would mostly be alone with fleeting relationships with women until he would meet someone he thought he could settle down with.

One night, when Sonny was about twenty-two years old, a working police officer in LA—and for the first time in his life, he was comfortable in his own skin—Raguel was visited by Archangel Gabriel in the deep subconscious of Sonny's mind while Sonny was dreaming. The assumption was that Sonny would be unaware of the meeting because he was dreaming about something else. This had been success-ful in the past when Michael had spoken to Raguel while Sonny's grandfather visited him to say goodbye. The angels sat on a park bench on a sunny day in a corner of Sonny's mind. Prophetic dreams were a special skill of Gabriel's. Gabriel was telling Raguel how to frame a prophetic dream for Sonny to warn him of imminent danger on patrol calls and thwart the forces of darkness' plans.

Both angels had underestimated Sonny's subconscious. Sonny became aware of the dream he was having of a subroutine running in his mind—another dream in progress, if you will. All of a sudden, he was conscious of the dream he was having of being on a roller coaster. He looked up and vanished from being a spectator of that dream to being part of the meeting between Archangel Gabriel and Raguel, standing in a park on a sunny day looking at two angels on a bench, wings and all. Both angels glowing with their respective purple and golden light, they were as shocked as he was. He was not supposed to be there. Archangel Gabriel looked at Rags with an astonishing expression, which matched Sonny's face. Nothing was said as the three were frozen momentarily. Gabriel disappeared, and Raguel remained, continuing the eye contact with Sonny briefly before Sonny awoke. When he did awake from the dream at about 6:00 a.m., he knew this was not going to be a fleeting memory. He was up. He was charged with an energy and an enlightened knowledge that angels were real. This was going to stay with him like the memory of his grandfather's visitation in his dream when he was ten years old.

Archangel Michael was very direct that Sonny was not to discover the incarnation, but Archangel Gabriel had to report what happened to Archangel Michael. At the highest level of heaven, Gabriel approached Michael to report what happened when he contacted Raguel while Sonny was sleeping. He explained that he distracted Sonny's first level of subconscious by putting him in a dream about being on a roller coaster. He told Archangel Michael that he then met with Raguel in a deeper level of subconscious. Michael was not happy but impressed that Sonny could reach into his deepest subconscious to crash a meeting between two angels in his mind while in the middle of a dream. They spoke, and it was understood that Sonny had developed further than expected and the time had come to be more overt about his spiritual potential. It was time to interfere with the watchers, especially Azazel and Lilith.

Azazel and Lilith were busy doing what they do best—hanging around bars and places where drugs were openly used, whispering in ears, and causing mayhem. One of their favorite jump-ins was during the moment of conception of a child. The child, forever marked with a red aura, was basically an open invitation for a walk-in without any of the foreplay demons would have to go through with other people. Generally angels and demons are the only beings that can see this red glow. Does the mark always result in the corruption of a marked person's soul? No, but it's a beacon to try. Chaos and the corruption of mankind were the watchers' goals, and they were succeeding. Very soon, after seeing Gabriel and Rags in his dream, Sonny started having dreams about demons possessing people and doing awful shit. This triggered the struggles he had as a child, but these dreams were different. Sonny wasn't the main character in these dreams. It was like he was watching a movie, a spectator. At first, Sonny didn't make the connection that these dreams were actually premonitions of events that were yet to come and dismissed the aftereffects as déjà vu. Until…

It was around 1995. LA cops had to park their personal cars on city streets a couple of blocks from assigned precincts when arriving at work. Sonny had moved around in the last four to five years but was stationed in Burbank. He was on swing shift, 3:00 p.m. to 1:00 a.m. This was a tough time for Sonny because, after coming home from work one night after a swing shift, he discovered Dino had passed away alone in the garage. Dino always met Sonny at the door when he got home, wagging his tail and truly happy to see Sonny. On this occasion, when Sonny got home, Dino wasn't there. Sonny knew instantly. He searched the house and found him deceased in the garage.

Sonny lay next to Dino, crying his eyes out, telling him, "Daddy loves you. Daddy loves you."

Even though he'd only had Dino for about five years, this was a special bond. Sonny would later discover that the cause of death was his stomach twisting. A common thing for big dogs, but Sonny felt like Dino was taken from him prematurely.

Sonny gathered his strength and went back to work. Shortly thereafter, one sunny summer day at about two thirty, he parked his car a couple of blocks away as usual and began walking on the sidewalk to the station. Sonny was in civilian clothes because he liked to get changed at work. Cops' personal cars took less damage if they weren't seen getting out of them wearing a police uniform. There was a woman walking about ten feet in front of him, going in the same direction. She was well dressed and attractive. She looked like an attorney or something, gray business suit with a skirt and blazer and long dark hair, and walked with confidence. At first, Sonny thought it was just the sun reflecting off the sidewalk, but she appeared to have a reddish glow. Okay, now she really had his attention. Sonny saw an apparition on her right side. All those movies about ghosts told him this looked like a ghost. It was a scrawny female-looking ghost with long dark hair. It whispered in the woman's right ear, and then suddenly the woman sidestepped into the street into oncoming traffic and was struck by a large SUV. Sonny screamed no, but the woman was killed instantly. The ghost laughed and disappeared. Sonny awoke in a cold sweat. This dream was emotionally charged, not like a regular dream. It bothered him, but he had to go to work and didn't have time to analyze it.

He got ready and jumped in his car and headed to work. He parked in a usual spot on the street and started on foot to work. While passing a little coffee shop he frequented, an attractive woman exited the shop and turned right to walk in the same direction as Sonny. She smiled and said good morning, and for a second, it didn't hit Sonny that she was the woman with the red glow from his dream. He was still flattered that she took the time to say good morning. He had a backpack slung over one shoulder, cop boots on, and the cop sunglasses. He was parked a couple of blocks from a police station. It wasn't hard to deduce what his profession was. As they approached an intersection, it dawned on Sonny, and the events of his dream hit him. She did have an iridescent red glow. She started to slow down and turned her head to the right for no reason. Sonny's adrenaline surged, and his body was full of electricity. He closed the distance to intervene, unlike in his dream where he just shouted no. The apparition appeared. It was there. He saw it, just like the dream. His goosebumps were as big as golf balls. He almost couldn't talk. But he had seen this before, so he wasn't frozen. Just as the evil ghost began to whisper in the woman's ear, Sonny took the woman's left arm and spun her toward him, which startled her, but she smiled to see Sonny.

He said, "Excuse me. I thought you were about to trip and fall into the street."

The woman's red glow faded away. She smiled and continued walking. The apparition made eye contact with Sonny and took note that Sonny's eyes were shimmering with purple sparkle. The watcher gave an evil look and disappeared.

Sonny had always known he was different. There had always been signs. All the supernatural events of his life flashed in his mind culminating at this moment. He had seen two angels in a dream recently. He just had a premonition and stopped a watcher from killing some random woman he'd never met. But was he on some demon radar now? He was nervous and scared and needed answers right now! But who can you talk to about having the gift of prophecy who wouldn't think you are crazy? He was a police officer, and he liked and needed his job. He started to rationalize it away as coincidence. But the watchers took Sonny seriously. Lilith returned to Abaddon to report what she had seen to Azazel and Lucifer. Azazel was Lucifer's top lieutenant. Sonny was considered a person of interest in the past, but now he was a priority. They were aware that he was a descendant of Moses, but now they knew how he was saved from death when he was five years old. He was incarnate with an angel. But who? How high did this go? It was time for them to make another attempt on his life. His would not be some random drive-by on a police officer. They wanted it to be brutal and up close. This meant an edged weapon. This meant violence.

Sonny got a call about a disturbance in a warehouse district. People would rent out large storage facilities and use them to party because it was cheap and not a residence. Usually the cops would show up and give warnings and not come back. Cops got the nickname One Time because they always used to say, "If we have to come back here one more time…"

Anyway, Sonny got a call of a noise disturbance on a Friday at about 10:00 p.m. He parked a few storage containers away and got out of his car. As he exited, he turned around and looked behind himself, as was his habit for officer safety. It was pitch black, and he couldn't see anything. But something grabbed his arms. Then he felt the cold reality of sharp steel stabbing him repeatedly in his upper torso. His mind went to his mental filing cabinet for a frame of reference, but there was nothing there.

We've all heard the principle that your brain has two choices when confronted with a shocking new experience—fight or flight. Well, there is actually a third: freeze. The first instinct is to freeze, and that was what happened to Sonny.

He awoke frozen in his bed with some kind of audible yell. His girlfriend awoke and was about as comforting as a proctologist with big hands. It was a dream, a fucking scary one. But was it a premonition or just a nightmare? Sonny's girlfriend, Anne, was beautiful but had the emotional depth of a teaspoon. She was with Sonny because he was a good-looking guy that made decent money and cops had that pension at the end of the rainbow. Sonny was with her because she was sexy and made him feel special, like the way that driving an expensive sports car makes a young man feel. So in a way, they were both using each other, I guess. Anne was from Hawaii, the daughter of a Caucasian father in the navy and a Hawaiian mom. She was gorgeous. She was about five feet, four inches, and athletic with long dark hair. Heads turned wherever she went. She spent most nights at Sonny's house although she did not technically live with him. She was about twenty-five, and he was about thirty years old at this time. She was the kind of girl that always had a boyfriend but was always cultivating a possible new boyfriend if it looked like the grass was greener elsewhere.

A couple of weeks later, Sonny got another call to a warehouse district for a noise disturbance. This time, he parked farther away and right up against a building. He thought to himself that he didn't leave himself much room to get out, but whatever. He rationalized this red flag away for some reason and carried on with business. It was pitch dark, and a lighted phone booth caught his attention that was about thirty yards away in the distance. He usually looked behind himself when exiting a car, but this time, he didn't because he was focused on the phone booth. In the darkness, he felt something grab his arms as he shut his car door, but he couldn't see a face or make out the shape of a person. His brain went to his filing cabinet, and he instantly recognized the situation because of the dream a couple of weeks prior. He began fighting furiously, kicking and punching to get free. He was able to fight instead of freeze because his mind had a reference point now. He awoke punching the air and yelling. It was another dream. Anne, of course, awoke as well. Gabriel, it seemed, had been vigilant, monitoring the plans of the watchers. Sonny would not have to wait very long to discover that these dreams would prepare him for what was to come.

A short time later, Sonny was working a swing shift in the north part of Burbank. He had just had his dinner break at Anne's house, which was in the south part of town. He decided to stop into a community center while he was in the area to play basketball (on duty) with at-risk youth. A call came out of a disturbance at an apartment complex nearby. The reporting person said that her neighbor was at her door screaming at her to come outside and acting erratic. Sonny volunteered for the call because he was in the area. Sonny arrived and saw a woman matching the description standing in front of the building. He made contact with her and introduced himself. She was evasive and agitated. Sonny asked her what her name was.

She replied, "It doesn't matter."

Sonny told her that, if they were going to talk, he'd like to know what her name was. She had both hands in her pockets and was looking around generally indifferent to Sonny's presence. The woman told Sonny that he could call her Fay. About this time, another officer arrived on the scene, an older female officer named Patricia; but people called her Pat. Sonny and Pat took standard triangulation positions of interview with Fay while Sonny did the talking (an officer on either side of a suspect about an arm and a half distance away). Sonny was pretty tapped into seeing people's auras but didn't see any red around Fay. Something was wrong.

Fay grew tired of Sonny's questions and started to walk away. Sonny was on the left, and Pat was on his right. As Sonny reached out to take control of Fay's right arm, she pulled away and took her right hand out of her coat pocket. Sonny missed her arm, got air, and was leaning forward. Fay had a long serrated knife in her hand, which came down on Sonny's head first, partially severing the ocular nerve on his left eye. Then she stabbed him through the top of his trapezius and down into his chest. The last stab went through his left arm and into his left latissimus dorsi. It was a fast and violent attack, three stabs in milliseconds.

Fay then went after Pat. She pulled Pat by the hair with her left hand, bending her over at the waist. Fay got one hit on Pat—a through and through across the trapezius but not down into the chest like Sonny. Fay's hand was raised high with the knife in it. She was coming down on the back of Pat's neck, and this would have surely killed Pat. Sonny drew his weapon and shot Fay, stopping the murder of his partner. He fired a couple of more times while moving in a circular direction to avoid hitting Officer Pat. There was no sound of the gunshots in Sonny's ears. The whole thing happened in slow motion. Fay went down to one knee but still had the knife in her hand and was a couple of feet from Officer Pat. By now, Pat had drawn her sidearm. She aimed at Fay's torso and fired one shot, striking Fay. This shot Sonny heard. It was like he was in a dream, and this shot woke him up.

Three shots and three hits one handed with one eye working. Fay stabbed Sonny three times in the blink of an eye but was only able to stab officer Pat once before Sonny reacted. This was impossible. How could Sonny have possibly reacted that quickly? Answer: because Gabriel had prepared him with the two dreams so that his mind was ready for this event.

Sonny got on his handheld radio and called dispatch, "LA 0043, I've been stabbed, and Officer Patricia has also been stabbed. The suspect is down and not moving." Sonny said, "We need ambulances immediately."

A sergeant who wasn't even on scene canceled the ambulances. We'll just call him Sergeant Stupid.

"Negative. LA doesn't allow medics in there until the scene is secured." (Azazel whispered in Sergeant Stupid's ear.)

Sonny was bleeding internally on the side of the road in front of a crappy apartment complex, and not knowing if he was bleeding out or if Officer Pat was, Sonny took off his uniform shirt and bulletproof vest to assess the damage. He was clearly hurt worse than Pat. She told Sonny to sit down on the curb. No one could see the apparition, Lilith dancing around Sonny as he was bleeding out. The watchers celebrated their victory over the angels protecting Sonny and the bloodline of Moses. They had finally got him. Sonny could hear sirens blaring in the distance and knew help was close. He saw the red-and-blue flashing lights of a marked unit arriving. It was the most relieving thing he'd ever seen, two guys from the gang unit that he knew, Mike and Tommy. Mike was on the SWAT team and was a tactical thinker. Mike heard Sergeant Stupid say "Don't let the medics in," so he made the decision to put Sonny and Pat in their police car and take them to the hospital. It was only about five miles to the closest hospital, but it seemed like forever.

When they got to the ER, Sonny had no shirt on and was instructed to lie on the gurney. The cold metal touching his skin hit him with the reality of what just happened. Medical staff were talking about the female arriving with gunshot wounds, and Sonny began to panic, thinking he had accidentally shot Pat. He asked questions, but medical staff were frantic doing what they needed to do. Finally a nurse quietly and gently addressed Sonny. She told him Patricia was right next to him, and she was not shot. She told him to relax and let them do what they needed to do. Apparitions not visible to human eyes were everywhere. Watchers, angels, and humans who hadn't crossed over crowded the emergency room. Watchers with their red auras and angels with golden auras equalized the ER, concern from the angels and sadistic celebrating from the watchers.

Uriel, the angel of light and justice, known as the fourth angel, appeared; and the very present red glows in the room were drowned out by his light, except for Azazel's. His red glow diminished but didn't disappear. Azazel wanted to wait and see what happened. Uriel's wings were massive, and the light emanating was like the sun. Uriel had a history of dispensing justice without mercy. He was an arch-angel, but he also had a mean streak. Most of the watchers left quickly, like a shooting in a downtown nightclub in Hollywood. Some covered their eyes. They were terrified. Uriel was one of the most powerful angels ever created by God. To even brush against his wing by a demon meant the demon would instantly turn to smoldering dust. They were right to be terrified.

Uriel approached Sonny and scanned his body. He could see the knife and the trajectory of each stab wound. Sonny's heart was beating, and Uriel could see the left and right ventricles and his aorta. Uriel saw that the knife missed Sonny's aorta by about an inch and also missed his lungs. Uriel smiled as he placed his hand on Sonny's head, and an instant peace fell over Sonny. Uriel looked over at Azazel and disappeared. But Azazel was still there. Why?

Normally a watcher couldn't penetrate Sonny's mind because Raguel could ward them off. But Sonny's mor-phine drip was just inserted into a vein. Narcotics were weakening for Sonny, just like alcohol or drugs would be. He was hypersensitive to it. As the drip penetrated Sonny's body, Azazel entered Sonny's mind. This was why he stuck around when Uriel arrived. Sonny was out cold, conscious and subconscious, basically unprotected. Suddenly Sonny was seated on a park bench watching his eight-year-old nephew, Austin, playing with other kids on a playground. Austin was his older sister's, Marcy's, son. Marcy and Sonny had grown close, and she was one of the only people who knew about his dreams and that Sonny was different. She knew about his gift of prophecy and believed. All of the kids had their usual refreshing golden auras except a little girl with a red glow. She approached Sonny with red eyes and a red aura and sat down next to him on the bench.

"We're going to get you, ya know," said Azazel.

Sonny replied, "Why? Why me?"

Azazel's voice was not that of the little girl that he was physically representing himself to be, but it wasn't deep and crazy demonic like in the movies either. Remember, Azazel was calm and calculating, the devil's right hand. It was an adult male voice coming out of the face of a ten-year-old girl. Maybe he felt that was creepy enough.

Azazel asked rhetorically, "Don't you know? You are the descendant of Moses and Zipporah. You were marked for death, as are all the children of Amram and Jochebed," parents of Moses. Aaron and Miriam were Moses's siblings.

Azazel told Sonny watchers had been trying to kill him since he was five years old, successfully once. This time, they came within one inch.

Sonny asked, "Why am I still alive then?"

Azazel replied, "Ask your friend Rags."

The same time this conversation was taking place, Sonny's body lay still on a hospital gurney. Medical staff and police officers were all around Sonny. A police officer was just nearly stabbed to death. It was kind of a big deal. The angel Saraqael (Sariel) was witness to that sneaky bastard Azazel entering Sonny's mind when the morphine hit his system. She couldn't see what was going on, but she knew it wasn't good. Sariel was a beautiful female angel with long blond hair and a sword that would flame when drawn from her scabbard. Sariel was tall with silver armor and beautiful pinkish-white wings. She was fast, real fast. All angels could teleport, but Sariel could travel at superhuman speed in whatever form she took.

Sariel whispered in a police officer's ear, "Wake him up."

Instantly the officer told the doctor to wake Sonny up. The doctor told the officer it was better for Sonny to be unconscious right now.

Again Sariel whispered in the officer's ear, "We have questions for him. Do it."

The doctor started injecting what it took to bring Sonny to consciousness about the same time Azazel told Sonny to ask Rags.

Sonny regained consciousness, and his supervisor asked him the typical questions: Were there any outstanding suspects? Did he want a lawyer? Did he remember the basics of what happened? He remembered, but his thoughts were on the dream he just had and being threatened by a little girl with a man's voice. The ER doctor in charge stepped in and told the officers, if they were done, he'd like to speak to his patient. The doctor told Sonny the blade missed his aorta by one inch. He was lucky. But it did penetrate the nerve ball in his left armpit, and he would feel this day forever. He also might lose part of his left triceps from nerve damage, and the stab to the head hit the ocular nerve of his left eye. The doctor could have stopped at the one-inch statement, as far as sonny was concerned. Azazel told him they missed killing him by one inch this time. Sonny asked the doctor what would happen if the knife clipped his aorta.

The doctor replied, "You would have bled out on the street."

Sonny sat in silence for a second and thought, *Who is Rags?*

Sonny was released from the hospital the next day, as was Officer Patricia. Patricia called him the day they were released (they were released at different times). She thanked Sonny for saving her life and doing what he did. They never spoke again. His arm was in a sling, and he would be on administrative leave with pay while the investigation was conducted. Luckily there were witnesses that corroborated Sonny's and Patricia's statements. The press was all over the incident: "POLICE KILL WOMAN. Why did Officer D'Antoni fire three times? Are the police officers racist?"

A lot of preconceived notions about Sonny came out. Numerous police stereotypes were thrown at Sonny: another White racist cop with a silver-spoon background kills a helpless citizen. Sonny, the grandson of an Italian immigrant who obtained citizenship by fighting for the US in WWII, whose best friends were Black and Korean, who grew up with government cheese and food stamps, and who was threatened by the mob was a "silver-spoon White racist." Ironic.

The police chief didn't defend the officers at all, merely saying in a press conference, "Let's allow the process to play itself out."

The political climate in 2000 was that it was advantageous to publicly eviscerate a police officer whenever possible. At first, Sonny was okay; but after the months on admin leave and being called a murderer by the public, he started to worry. There were some cops doing bad things, and all cops paid the price for it. Sonny did for sure—at home for three months wearing the title "homicide suspect." He was ready to go back to work; but his injuries, scar tissue, and nerve damage would never go away. Patricia would never wear a police uniform again. She had almost twenty-four years in the department and found her way to medical retirement, collateral damage in the watchers' attempt to murder Sonny. Only one officer above the rank of sergeant (Lieutenant Steve Potts) called him while he was on admin leave / recovering to see if he was doing okay. Steve was a cops' cop. He was from Oakland. He was tough, but he bled blue. Steve Potts practiced martial arts like Sonny, and there was mutual respect. Everyone else wanted to avoid getting burned by any political fire that Sonny was in. It was bad enough that he was literally stabbed within one inch of his life but saved Pat's life, and now he was abandoned by his police department. Demoralizing was an understatement for how Sonny was treated. Imagine behaving like a hero but being treated like a zero.

Sonny was about thirty years old and decided it was time to start a family. His girlfriend, Anne, had him believing that she loved him and not just the status of being a police officer with a stable job and great retirement. Sonny met Anne at a nightclub. He was there after work with a couple of friends and was leaving after a night of drinking and dancing. Anne caught his eye, and Sonny adjusted his course and walked over to her and introduced himself. The two hit it off and danced all night. They dated for about six to eight months prior to the stabbing. He was home for three months on admin leave, and he and Anne had plenty of alone time. Bingo, Anne got pregnant with their first son. In truth, he would have married her no matter what. He loved Anne. He was blind to any narcissism. Within six months of the stabbing, he was engaged with a baby on the way.

Angels and demons alike had left him alone, and he started to rationalize the events at the hospital as hallucinations. Anne was basking in the attention of the engagement and pregnancy. Sonny was finally cleared of any wrongdoing in the stabbing/shooting. An article in the back of the newspaper clearing him by the district attorney was the only press coverage of the vindication. The DA acknowledged that the fast reactions of Sonny saved Pat's life. Still there was no celebration and no appropriate recognition given by the top police administration. Patricia and others recommended Sonny for the Medal of Valor for his actions. The chief, Jerry Plummer, an asshat with political aspirations, told Pat that he could not publicly award an officer the Medal of Valor for killing a woman of color and Sonny was just responding to training. What a dick. In a small not-publicized ceremony, Sonny got the Purple Heart and the Medal of Meritorious Service. The Medal of Merit was a complete slap in the face to Sonny. It was a joke. It had been given out for mapping the streets of apartment complexes or getting curbs painted red in high drug-dealing areas. But Sonny was cleared for duty and ready to get back to work. He had a baby on the way and was getting married.

Sonny knew though. He knew his dreams were real. He knew he was on demons' radar for some reason. He knew he had seen ghosts. He knew he had the divine gift of prophecy. He tried several times in his life to shut that part of him off and pretend it was not real. Hadn't he been through enough? There were always ghosts around Sonny. Sonny had a spiritual light that was a beacon for spirits everywhere who just wanted to be seen or heard again. There were always apparitions walking around the house. Faucets were turning on and off. There was knocking all the time. Usually it was harmless. He learned to live with it, but other people in his life had to adjust to it. Anne would see or hear things from time to time. It was unsettling to her, but usually she was okay.

On one occasion, Anne had a dream that she was possessed by a demon. She was floating above her body, looking down at herself dreaming and being thrashed on the ceiling. She awoke, and her body was in the same position that it was in the dream. Needless to say, this completely freaked her out. She wanted to sell the house and move. Sonny knew it wasn't the house; it was him. But what could he do? Sonny was worried that the spiritual open door that he was would be genetic. Would it pass to his children? His pregnant fiancé just had a dream that she was possessed. What the fuck?

How do I turn this shit off? he thought to himself.

They got married and stayed in the house. About five months later, Anne gave birth to their first child, Luke Santino D'Antoni. Sonny wanted the boy to have his name so he would know how important he was to him forever. And since Sonny's first name is Lucas and he went by that name for the first part of his life, it seemed appropriate.

Sonny soon received the answer to his question, Would his children carry his burden of spiritual duty? By the time Luke could coo and respond playfully (six months), he would giggle and coo to no one that was visible. It was obvious that he was interacting with someone or something. Sonny was scared. He did not want this burden or calamity to befall Luke or any future children. Sonny prayed every night, the same four prayers he'd said since he could remember. On a particular night, where Luke interacted with unknown invisible energy, Sonny prayed.

"Our Father, who art in heaven, hallowed be the name. Thy kingdom come. Thy will be done on earth as it is in heaven. Give us this day our daily bread and forgive us our trespasses as we forgive those who trespass against us, and lead us not into temptation but deliver us from evil. Amen.

"Hail Mary, full of grace. The Lord is with thee. Blessed art thou amongst women and blessed is the fruit of thy womb, Jesus. Holy Mary, mother of God, pray for us sinners now and at the hour of our death. Amen.

"Apostles' Creed. I believe in God the Father Almighty, creator of heaven and earth, and in Jesus Christ, his only Son, our Lord, who was conceived by the Holy Spirit, born of the Virgin Mary, suffered under Pontius Pilate, and was crucified, died, and was buried. On the third day, he rose again from the dead in fulfillment of the scriptures. He will come again in glory to judge the living and the dead, and his kingdom will have no end. I believe in the Holy Spirit, the holy Catholic Church, the communion of saints, the forgiveness of sins, the resurrection of the body, and the life of the world to come. Amen.

"Act of Contrition. Oh, my God, I am heartily sorry for offending you, and I detest all my sins because of the just punishments but, most of all, because they offend you, my God. I firmly resolve with the help of your grace to do no more and avoid the near occasions of sin. Amen."

Then Sonny would thank God for his many blessings and ask him to protect his family. He would ask for specific help if a family member was going through a particular struggle or challenge. First was always his son, Luke, then his wife, his mother, sisters, etc. Now it was time to speak candidly with God.

"What have you been preparing me for? Please don't put Luke through life as I've had. Please send an angel to help me. Please protect us from the evil forces that have targeted my lineage."

Sonny got his answer that night. The archangel Gabriel gave him a vision in a dream. It went like this.

He stood in a dark place. It was desolate and barren, a vast turbulent nothingness except a gate of fire that appeared before him. What was beyond the gate was obscured and dark. It was a semicircle of fire that was about as big as the Reno Arch. There were no creatures of any kind that stood guard at the gate, nothing to indicate that this was the entrance to hell. No signs or welcome committee, just an unmonitored gate. Sonny knew that he had to enter to rescue Luke. In his dream, he just knew that Luke was captive in there somewhere. Sonny was strangely confident and unafraid. He had a bright golden glow, like the glow that Uriel had when he came to Sonny in the hospital after he had been stabbed, just not quite as bright. Sonny felt a presence with him, a familiar soul that he had known his whole life but had never spoken to.

He heard a calming voice say, "Let's go get your son."

Remember, Archangel Michael instructed Raguel not to make his presence known to Sonny when Azazel and Lilith tried to kill Sonny when he was five years old, and Raguel saved his life by becoming incarnate with him. But things had changed. Sonny had been trained spiritually his entire life to have the energy and strength to comprehend a mere glimpse of God's plan and the lineage of Moses. Now there was another son born of Moses's DNA, and the demons were certainly going to step their game up. Sonny did not see Raguel, but he knew he was not alone. Sonny walked confidently toward the gate and entered hell. As he passed through the gate, he could see what was on the other side, souls being openly tormented and tortured by demons and grotesque creatures like hellhounds and bound at their legs and feet and openly mutilated with edged weapons. It was gruesome. Yeah, it was hell.

Flames and lava flowed like a river, and there were small sections on either side where souls were isolated from each other like separate prison cells without bars. Sonny looked up and saw winged creatures flying above like small dragons that were tearing flesh from the bones of poor souls that were trapped there. It took a second to absorb what he was seeing, and it was most certainly disorienting. But the creatures that stood out were giant humanoid-like creatures. They were huge, ten to fifteen feet tall, with underdeveloped wings. The wings were mutilated and too small for any effective use. They were menacing looking and ill tempered. Unlike the demons that were tormenting souls, the giants appeared to be eating people.

But then Sonny saw a pattern, a route to navigate. The river of fire flowed downward to other areas. He saw a light like his own off in the distance that was like a beacon, giving him his path to Luke. As soon as Sonny passed through the gate, it was like someone turned on the light. Demons and creatures alike turned their attention to Sonny.

Raguel told Sonny, "Fear not any of these unholy creatures, for no tooth or claw will penetrate your skin. You are protected by the One of Most High."

All manner of visually terrifying creatures sped toward Sonny, except the giants. They kept to themselves, spread out in the area eating and grunting. Sonny was unfazed by their approach. He began walking next to the river of fire toward Luke's light without fear. Demons, hellhounds, and winged monsters thrust themselves at Sonny from all angles, but like a force field of light, they bounced off his energy and vaporized. They weren't just repelled by his light; they were destroyed. As he made his way along the river, fewer and fewer monsters attempted to attack Sonny until they cowered upon his approach. He saw the giants on his way, but they continued to eat like gluttons and ignored Sonny.

Finally Sonny arrived at the light that had been guiding him. He saw that there were two teenage boys that were bound by the hands and feet. They appeared to be about fourteen and sixteen years old respectively. There were two giants nearby, and these two were not indifferent to the presence of Sonny or the two teenage boys. Both boys had a glowing light that ascended upward and out of hell. The boys' lights merged together as they went up, which made it appear as if the two lights were one. The older boy was Luke. Sonny immediately recognized his soul. He was tall and thin with curly brown hair and was the spitting image of Sonny when he was about sixteen. Luke exuded intelligence, like he could do calculus in his sleep.

The other boy was Sonny's second son, who was yet to be born. He was clearly manifesting as younger than Luke but was bigger. He was taller and thicker than Luke, muscular and bigger boned. He was darker skinned like Anne, with bright-green eyes. Anne was not even pregnant yet. Luke was only about a year old. Sonny knew this boy was his son. Sonny and his sons had an eternal contract to be soldiers of God that traces back to Amram and Jochebed. The two giants made eye contact with Sonny and began to walk toward the two boys.

One of the giants spoke to Sonny and said, "Son of Jochebed and Moses, we are the Nephilim, eternal adversaries of your blood."

They were salivating at the mouth, large jagged teeth with giant heads that could swallow a person whole with one bite. Sonny was about thirty feet away, and his body began to take flight. He rose from the ground as easily as a feather is whisked away in the wind. The was not the first time he had ever flown. Gabriel had taught him to fly in his dreams as a young child, and by now, it was natural for him. He flew to right in front of his sons, stopping the giants' advance. Sonny's inner light commanded the area as he touched down to the ground after his flight. The two giants attempted to continue their advance but could not step into Sonny's light. Sonny unbound his sons while telling them that everything was going to be okay. Neither of the kids was erratic or irrational, which would be the appropriate human emotional response given the situation.

Luke looked at his father with pride and said, "I knew you'd come for me and Joshua."

Sonny looked at the teenager that was yet to be born and said, "Hello, Joshua, let's go home."

Sonny took his sons by the arms, and all three began to ascend upward, not requiring walking out of hell on foot as it was necessary for Sonny to find them. Sonny awoke with peace and confidence similar to that of when he had the dream as a young child when he was in a river of positive energy with all animals of the earth flowing to heaven.

He opened his eyes and couldn't wait to tell Anne about it, but she was already up. She was standing in the door-way to the bathroom, holding something in her hand. She was kind of disheveled in her pajamas and clearly hadn't showered yet. She looked like she was in shock, half happy but half concerned. Then it dawned on Sonny that she was holding an at-home pregnancy test. They looked at each other for a moment without speaking until Anne broke the silence.

"I'm pregnant."

Sonny jumped to his feet and embraced Anne. She was kind of in shock and a little surprised that Sonny was that happy about it, which converted her fears to happiness pretty quickly. As the two held each other, Sonny said, if it was a boy, he'd like to name him Joshua and whatever middle name Anne wanted. Anne loved the name Joshua and wanted his middle name to be after her dad. It wouldn't be long before Joshua Donald D'Antoni would come into this world.

After the shock of that conversation sunk in and they started about their normal morning routine, Sonny began to reflect on his vision. What were the meanings? The fact that he was going to have another son and his wife was pregnant again, what the baby's name was, was a glaring truth; but what else? Was he being prepared for something in this lifetime or in a war for heaven after he left this world? He did awake with positivity and peace in the knowledge that heaven had his back and this pursuit of him and his children by dark forces would continue. Sonny was raised Catholic and prayed daily, but he didn't go to church every Sunday. It was a Saturday morning, and Sonny called a Catholic parish in Pasadena called Holy Cross. A priest who said his name was Father Joel answered the phone. He said that he would be happy to meet with Sonny the next day, Sunday morning, before the Masses started for the day.

The next day, at about 7:00 a.m., Sonny arrived at Holy Cross. The parking lot was empty, and all of the lights were off. He knocked on the door, and a couple of minutes later, Father Joel answered the door. Father Joel invited Sonny in, and they talked in a couple of empty pews of the church. Father Joel was in his midforties but presented himself with his mannerisms and speech of someone much older. He was about five feet, ten inches, with dark hair. And he was in good physical shape. He was wearing typical priest attire with a red sash. Sonny explained to Father

Joel that he hadn't been to church in a long time and he had been through a lot, but he had faith. Father Joel was patient and kind. He told Sonny that this wasn't going to be a where-have-you-been speech but quite the opposite; it was going to be a welcome-back conversation.

Father Joel said, "Let's get started with your confession."

Sonny explained that he was not there for a formal confession but that he had questions about Moses.

Father Joel said, in a nutshell, Moses was a good man that was given a very difficult task by God. But God walked with him on his path, and he was never alone. But more specifically, Moses was the son of Amram and Jochebed. He had a brother, Aaron, and a sister named Miriam. He later married a woman named Zipporah. They had two sons named Gershom and Eliezer. Moses was touched by God and empowered to deliver the people of Israel from slavery in Egypt. Of course, he spoke to God on Mount Horeb's "burning bush" and got his marching orders for how to free his people and not to fear, for God was with him.

Sonny said that he was familiar with the historical facts but was more interested in what were the powers and burdens that God had bestowed upon him. Father Joel said that Moses's relationship with God started with his mother placing Moses in the Nile River and set upon a path of danger to avoid being massacred by the pharaoh, who had ordered all firstborn Jewish sons to be executed. It was not clear if it was the queen or the queen's daughter who found Moses, but he was adopted by the royal family. For most of his life, his true lineage was unknown to him. But God cultivated the relationship for his ultimate task that was in God's plan and the role that Moses would play. Moses had guardian angels that would place Moses in positions where he would have to learn and develop emotional courage and strength. He also frequently worked on construction projects that strengthened his body. Moses was given prophetic dreams, and later the events of the dream would come true. Angels were said to speak to him in his dreams when he was asleep, and he would get instinctual nudges. It was believed that Moses killed a brutal Egyptian slave master shortly after discovering that he was an adopted Jew and left Egypt.

Moses returned to Egypt after speaking to God on Mount Horeb to free his people at God's direction.

Sonny asked, "What powers was he given?"

"Well, apparently it would look something like what we call magic. He transformed his staff into a snake, which devoured Pharaoh Ramses's staff. He unleashed the ten plagues upon Egypt until Ramses was forced to release the slaves. He was basically a conduit for a millifraction of God's power."

Father Joel said that the congregation was about to arrive and the conversation would have to continue another day. Sonny asked if he could talk some more soon, and Father Joel agreed.

Sonny was working in the narcotics unit at the time and studying for the sergeant's test. Anne was pregnant with Joshua, and Luke was just over a year old. He had plenty on his plate, and he tried balancing it all. He was also reminded of his stabbing frequently. He felt unsettled frequently, and he wasn't sleeping well. He tried to explain this to Anne, but she told him that she didn't have time for his problems.

Nice wife, huh. He went to his general practitioner, but his doctor told him that wasn't his area of expertise. His doctor didn't believe in occasional tranquilizers like Xanax or Valium, so he prescribed an anxiety/depression medication that was more of a long-term commitment, a selective serotonin reuptake inhibitor or SSRI. Sonny started to take it, but in the first couple of weeks, he was even more anxious and jittery. Chemically altering his brain and weakening his system, Sonny wasn't knowingly volunteering to weaken his mind and leave Raguel powerless to help him, but that was what he was doing. In his mind, he didn't have much choice. He had to work and be a provider for his family. He didn't have time to let anxiety negatively affect his life, so he took the meds. He also did not want to appear weak to his wife. He had to be the alpha, or he would lose her respect.

Azazel saw this as an opportunity to fuck with Sonny. While Sonny was getting ready for work one afternoon, Sonny was shaving and looked in the mirror. It was like he was looking through someone else's eyes, like an out-of-body experience. His own face felt like he was looking at someone else. It temporarily freaked him out a bit as he shook his head. He mustered on with his day, but that seed was planted.

In the middle of the night, at about 3:00 a.m. that same day, while Sonny was asleep, Azazel whispered in his ear, "What if I'm not me anymore?"

That thought caused the mother of all panic attacks. The thought cascaded like an avalanche, like the snow on a mountain after an earthquake.

He thought, *What if I am losing my mind? What if I lose control? What damage can I do? What if I can't trust myself?*

All manner of irrational, illogical thoughts flooded his mind, and Raguel was powerless to help. It was like he wasn't even in the passenger's seat of Sonny's mind anymore. He was locked in the truck. The meds had dulled Sonny's neurotransmitters and blocked his positive synapses. The night seemed to last forever.

The next day, he called his doctor's office and was only able to talk to a nurse.

He explained what happened and asked, "Can a panic attack or hallucination result as a result of the meds?"

She responded as the puppet of Azazel, "No, that's not a result of your medication. You must have something else going on."

Laughing hysterically, Azazel whispered in the nurse's ear, and Sonny was sinking more into the belief that he was going crazy. This poor bastard. After all that he had been through in his life. Demons had harassed him for his entire life.

He thought, *My God, why have you forgotten me?*

The watchers were patient and relentless. Sonny took those meds and switched to two or three other kinds for about a year. He was still a good father and a loyal husband, doing what he had to do while his mind was focused on an activity or people. But when he was alone, the negative thoughts, body tremors, and irrational fears were always there waiting for him. Azazel, Lilith, and the other watchers were not successful at killing Sonny; but they had numbed his mind and activated a fear program that kept him tame and not doing God's work. His prophetic dreams had come to a halt. He didn't get nudges anymore. He was still Lucas

Santino D'Antoni but just wearing Sonny's face and going through the motions of being himself.

Unfortunately his wife was more concerned about being the center of attention, and the most important thing in her world was herself to give a shit about Sonny, biding her time as his wife as he worked and calculating how much she would be eligible to get from his retirement day by day as she stayed with him. Sonny was a prisoner of his own mind, in a cell that he voluntarily walked into. Sonny just got used to the punishment by Anne. Anne was incapable of saying "I'm sorry." It was not in her vocabulary to say "My bad," and nothing was ever good enough. Anne gave birth to Joshua about nine months later. About the same time, Sonny passed the sergeant's test and got promoted. He was working graveyard (10:00 p.m. to 8:00 a.m.). He'd come home as Anne was going to work and take care of the kids after working all night, trying to take naps with the boys when they slept. Then he would go back to work graveyard. As if walking on eggshells around Anne and worrying unnecessarily about his screen saver (*Am I still me?*) wasn't enough, he had to work as a new police sergeant, making command decisions and learning his new role.

The watchers didn't have to kill Sonny or make him get a traumatic brain injury like his grandfather. They didn't have to make him addicted to prescription drugs and abandon his family like his father. They harassed him until he thought he may have been losing his mind and dropped him off in a feedback loop with an unloving wife who was completely incapable of saying a nice thing about her husband. And yet Sonny continued to move forward and persevere. While Sonny worked graveyard, Anne had several affairs. Cunning narcissists rarely get caught. Every now and then, she would drink enough wine to sleep with Sonny, just to seem like she was still interested in him but emotionally punishing. Nothing was ever good enough. The ironic thing was Anne wasn't under the influence of the watchers. That's just who she was. She was the best player on the watchers' team, and she wasn't even on the payroll. The SSRIs were keeping Sonny sedated in brain fog, and it also diminished his energy and sex drive. It would have been different if he'd had a spouse he could confide in, but that just wasn't Anne.

Deep in his gut, he knew he was not himself. This wasn't the person he wanted or knew that he could be. Sonny had irrational fears and had to mentally fence with himself about the shoji thoughts, or he would dwell on why he'd had the thought. He tried to visualize his thoughts like clouds or trains and just let them pass by without grabbing them, but those techniques never seemed to help. He went back to his doctor. He'd been on these meds for almost two years (mostly without Anne's knowledge). He explained to Doc Hayle that the SSRIs helped with the anxiety, but he wasn't feeling anything, kind of like chemo for the emotional chemicals of the brain or looking out a dirty windshield. You can kind of see where you are going, but the picture isn't clear.

Doc Hayle told him, "In that case, here is a prescription for an occasional Xanax, and get off the other meds."

"Huh? Why didn't you say this two years ago, Doc?"

Within a couple of weeks, Sonny started to think more like himself. Sure, there were some withdrawals from the meds, and he was a little more hypervigilant. But he wasn't in a brain fog. Raguel got his passenger's seat back. Sonny hardly touched the tranquilizers. Then the thought hit him.

I should go back and talk to Father Joel.

He called Holy Cross, and Father Joel answered just like before. The following Sunday, he was knocking on the door to the church. Father Joel invited him in. It had been about two years since they had spoken. Sonny explained what had been going on with his life and some of the struggles. By this point in his life, Sonny was more willing to be transparent with his feelings and pretty much told Father Joel about his death at five years old, the prophetic dreams and the visions of his stabbing, and subsequent supernatural events that had happened to him. Father Joel was a patient listener and asked that they just focus on the dream he had walking into hell to rescue Luke the morning Anne told him she was pregnant. Sonny was ready to talk about that because he wasn't sure about all the meanings.

Father Joel asked Sonny how he felt when he awoke from the dream. That most likely would uncover God's intent for the dream. Sonny explained that he felt incredibly positive, like a warrior for God who need not fear any of the devil's tools. He knew that the devil had it out for Sonny, but God would protect him through the fight.

Father Joel said, "Isn't that ironic? That is how Moses felt before the tasks that our Savior set before him."

Sonny told Father Joel that he was empowered to walk into hell impervious to the devil's demons.

Father Joel asked, "What else?"

Sonny explained the dream and asked why he was called the son of Amram and Jochebed. "Is it possible that I am a descendant of Moses?"

Father Joel said, "Not much is documented about Moses's sons, Gershom and Eliezer, but it's a safe bet that they had kids."

Sonny asked, "What's the outcome of the kids when the father had been touched by God like Moses was?"

Father Joel explained that Moses was a conduit for God's power for the greater good, and God worked through Moses. So it wasn't really Moses's power but the Almighty's. That being said, some humans were blessed and tasked with the divine gift of prophecy and had a responsibility to use it for good.

Sonny cited example after example of visions that he had been given that came true, ultimately to the visions of his stabbing. Father Joel explained that, out of all the divine gifts, prophecy was the rarest. Moses was the most infamous prophet in the Bible.

Sonny asked, "What does this mean for my sons? Will they be pursued by the watchers as I had? Anne had seen ghosts in the house. She was giving Luke a bath the other day, and she and the baby saw the ghost of a man in a top hat walk by the bathroom door. The dog ran out of the bathroom and gave chase, and the ghost disappeared. Luke was interacting with spirits in his crib, and I had met Joshua in the dream where I walked into hell to save Luke. What does this mean for the boys? I did not want this burden for my sons!"

Father Joel told Sonny to prepare the boys for what they might face and keep no secrets about the challenges. Father Joel told Sonny, "The days of Lucifer transforming into a dragon and leading two hundred fallen angels against heaven and Archangel Michael piercing his body with a flaming sword, casting him into Abaddon, are long gone. The battle for mankind is the daily struggle to keep Lucifer from corrupting individual souls and keeping humans on the right paths. Every dream, every nudge that you act upon that saves a soul is in completion of your purpose, and someday that will be your sons' purpose as well. Like it or not, that is the burden of Moses's blood."

Sonny thanked Father Joel for his time and headed off to work.

Sonny's friend Brentavious Tinsley was in charge of an undercover narcotics unit in Pasadena. Brentavious was a stocky Black sergeant and was originally from Las Vegas. Neither he nor Sonny had a *Brady Bunch* childhood, so they got along. They had worked together in that unit a couple of years prior to them getting promoted. Brentavious knew about the nudges Sonny would get and the dreams he had before the shooting/stabbing. One rule of buying narcotics undercover is to control the location. Undercover officers were schooled that you never go in a residence, apartment, or motel. The transactions were done in public so that cover officers could monitor what was going on. Sonny saw the undercover officer Matt Becker walking into a second-story hotel in downtown Pasadena with a couple of drug dealers.

Sonny thought, *Don't fucking do that, Matt. Don't do it.*

A couple of seconds later, Sonny heard shots being fired, and the occupants of the room began evacuating the room, running from the area. Sonny stopped his patrol car and saw all of the plain-clothes officers that were watching the room from their hiding spots emerge and run toward the room. Detective Matt Becker had been shot and killed in that room in a drug deal gone bad. Sonny awoke. It was just a dream. But he had a vision. The visions were back. But what now? Father Joel told Sonny it was his responsibility to use the prophecies for good.

Sonny called Brentavious. He asked him if he had an undercover dope buy scheduled for today.

Brentavious said, yes, he did.

Sonny asked, "Was Matt Becker the UC?"

Brentavious said, "Yeah. How'd you know?"

Sonny told him to call off the op and Matt Becker was going to be killed in a botched undercover dope buy. Sonny told Brentavious he knew it sounded crazy, and he told him about the dream. Sergeant Tinsley canceled that operation, and he and his team did something else that night. Sonny 100 percent knew he had saved an officer's life, a lot like when he saved the woman from being pushed in the street by Azazel. But was he going to be back on the devil's radar? The giant Nephilim in the dream vowed to never give up coming after Sonny. Azazel also told Sonny they would never let him rest in the vision he had when he was on morphine after the stabbing. For about the last two years, he was voluntarily sedated with anxiety meds, but supernatural activity had subsided. Now he was back on the job for God, using the gifts he had been tasked with. It was time to go see Father Joel. It's not like he could talk to Anne about it. She was going to Las Vegas and Florida and was pretty much checked out of the marriage. Sonny was working the swing shift, and he thought he would stop by Holy Cross on his way to work.

It was about 2:00 p.m. when Sonny arrived. The church was busy. The 1:00 p.m. Mass had just let out, and there were a lot of people exiting the church. After a couple of minutes waiting in the lobby, the priest, who had just concluded Mass, had been in front of the church, shaking the parishioner's hands as they left. Sonny waited patiently, and when it appeared that the priest was free, Sonny approached him. He was an older man in his late sixties, and he had a thick Irish accent. His name was Father Robert, and he had white hair, wearing white and green robes. Sonny introduced himself, and the father did the same. Sonny told Father Robert that he had been to the church a couple of times (the last visit, recently) and had really great conversations with Father Joel and something happened today that he was really excited to tell Father Joel about. Father Robert said that there were two priests at this parish, he and another who was recently been reassigned to another parish.

Sonny said, "Okay, where did Father Joel get reassigned to?"

Father Robert said, "Well, funny thing is that the other priest was from Ghana, and his name was Father Nyaabila, not Father Joel."

Sonny said, "That's impossible," and described Father Joel to Father Robert. Sonny became animated and walked back in the lobby of the church and pointed to a section of pews, saying, "We sat right there and talked for hours twice."

Father Robert assured Sonny that there was no Father Joel at that parish. Father Robert could see that Sonny was upset and confused. Father Robert was calm and approached Sonny, placing his hand on Sonny's shoulder.

He asked Sonny, "Did Father Joel help you with what you were going through?"

Sonny replied, "Yes, yes, he did."

Father Robert told Sonny, "Then he fulfilled his contract with you, and it was time for you to move forward with the knowledge that you had been given."

Sonny thanked Father Robert for his time and headed to work.

As he was headed to work, thoughts swirled in his mind. How did he have conversations with a priest that wasn't real? After all that Sonny had been through in his life, his logical mind still tried to rationalize the supernatural experiences as explainable and plausible. Raguel, sitting in the passenger's seat of Sonny's mind, was shaking his head. Raguel couldn't communicate with Archangel Michael, Gabriel, Uriel, or even Joel without risking Sonny discovering his presence. Sonny's mind was almost there though. Joel was obviously sent to let Sonny know that he wasn't alone in this fight and explain some things. Now that Sonny's mind was free of sedative drugs, he was open to messages, nudges, and dreams again that he could act upon, as evidenced by saving Detective Becker. But Raguel knew this would not go unnoticed by the watchers either.

The watchers were definitely not going to forget that the line of Moses had two more sons to contend with in the future, in Luke and Joshua. He was right. The top watchers were meeting at that moment to get their orders from Lucifer himself.

Until now, Lucifer was content to allow Azazel to pursue and harass Sonny, but he had grown tired of Sonny interfering with his corruption of mankind. In a café in East Los Angeles, arriving one at a time, Azazel entered a restaurant and took a seat in a booth. Lilith arrived shortly thereafter and sat across from him. She asked Azazel why he had called her to be there. Azazel told her that this meeting was called by the boss. Lilith was a high-ranking watcher, but she usually got her orders from Azazel. The fact that Lucifer was coming made her unsettled. Azazel was calm, calculating, and smart. He also didn't lose his cool. Lucifer was a different story. He had a temper. He was unpredictable. Although they were on the same side, she did not enjoy being in his presence. Lucifer's temper was like a raging storm inside that he was constantly trying to hold back and contain. One false step in a conversation and a village would be burnt down. Lucifer also rarely appeared in human form and despised appearing as such, so he was already going to be pissed off. But this meeting couldn't take place in hell. There were archangels whose sole purpose was to monitor hell, and this meeting needed to be secret. Each person that entered the café drew the demons' attention, wondering if they were the devil.

Then entered an overweight teenage White girl, a very unassuming person that drew no one's attention except

Lilith and Azazel, dressed plainly in a T-shirt and jeans that the rest of the world would ignore, exactly as Lucifer wanted it. Other than glowing red eyes revealing a glimpse of the fire within and a generally unpleasant demeanor, nothing stood out about her at all. Lucifer had stepped into her body minutes earlier as she was on her way to school and diverted her destination to the café that Azazel and Lilith now occupy. (Remember that the children of a demon step-in, upon conception, have a faint red glow. The devil can walk into them easily without any corruption necessary first.) Lilith was basically pissing herself as Lucifer approached, and Azazel's normally calm expression changed to indicate the pucker factor he was feeling. Lucifer asked the pair if this seat was taken and motioned to sit in an empty space next to Lilith. They both nodded, and he sat down.

Lucifer looked into Lilith's eyes and said, "I hate these fucking humans. If you two had done your job, I wouldn't have to be here."

There was a brief moment of silence except for the noise of the café in the background.

Azazel broke the silence by saying, "He's had help."

Lucifer raised his fist and slammed it down on the café table and grunted angrily, which raised the attention of other patrons in the café as they saw this benign-looking teenage girl appear to scold two adults that she was sitting with. Lucifer took a breath and regained his composure. It would seem that the devil was not fond of excuses.

"Who? Who is helping him? You've killed this fucker twice, haven't you? Successfully once?"

Lilith said that they believed that he was saved by an angel incarnation when they killed Sonny when he was five years old.

Lucifer said that his spies in heaven had said no such thing.

"It wasn't one of the big four!" Lucifer exclaimed.

Azazel said it wouldn't have to be to save the child's life. Any angel that would not be missed could do it. It would not have to be a high-ranking angel. Lucifer said that he was growing intolerable in this descendant of Moses interfering with their activities. Lilith said that they have stopped his heart, stabbed him, and sedated him with anxiety meds; but somehow he kept doing God's work. The angels of heaven had been showing more interest in this one's survival than the previous descendants.

Lucifer asked, "What about the wife?"

Azazel said that she was a beautiful, emotionally abusive narcissist and couldn't care less if Sonny got hit by a car.

Lucifer replied, "Well, at least you've done something right."

Lilith said, "Actually that's just her. She's a punishing female Virgo."

Lucifer said he would find out who the angel incarnate was. In the meantime, he had two directions. Lucifer said, "Number one, start whispering in the wife's ear to turn Sonny away from his friends and family so he was alone." He wanted Sonny to feel alone and trapped to trigger more feelings of anxiety and less enthused about doing

God's work. "Then when he's good and depressed, have the wife leave him for some other man or woman. I don't care."

Azazel asked, "And the second thing?"

Lucifer replied, "The second thing just walked through the door."

All three looked up at the figure that just walked into the café. It was a man about six feet, four inches, wearing a gray hooded sweatshirt pulled up over his head. He was dark complected and had a mustache and beard. He looked disheveled like he had been walking a long time. He walked to the table and sat down next to the girl that was inhabited by Lucifer. He removed his hood as the three stared at him.

Lucifer said aloud, "You remember your brother Samjaya."

Samjaya was one of the original two hundred watchers at the time of Lucifer's rebellion. The other watchers delighted in fornicating with human women during the time of the first men/women. Samjaya warned them of God's wrath, but the two hundred did it anyway. They were obsessed with knowing what the feeling of sex was like with mortal women and disobeyed God's orders for angels to leave humans alone. The offspring of angels and mortal women were the giants that Sonny saw in hell called the Nephilim. The archangels Michael and Gabriel killed most of the Nephilim, but some survived and now called hell their home. They weren't angels nor humans, deformed and slow witted.

Samjaya did not agree with the desecration of God's female human creations and did not lie with mortal women. He did, however, pick the wrong team. He was friends and brothers with Lucifer, who used to be one of God's favorite angels. Lucifer despised mankind and was jealous that God favored mankind over his angelic creations. So he and the two hundred watchers betrayed their oaths to watch mankind and be guardians of God's creations of the earth. They attacked heaven and lost. For his betrayal, Archangel Michael confined Lucifer to hell and made his flesh reflect the ugliness within. His appearance in demonic form was hideous. The remaining watchers that were not killed in the battle were also sent to hell. There had been other watchers killed on earth by the big four—Michael, Gabriel, Raphael, and Uriel—since the rebellion. Archangel Uriel, the fourth angel, particularly delighted in the slaying of a watcher that was fucking with humanity. So what of Samjaya?

Samjaya did not lie with mortal women. He fathered no Nephilim. For his crime of aligning with Lucifer, God banished him to earth to live as a mortal but never succumbed to a mortal death until the end of days, the Apocalypse. God took away his wings and all of his angelic powers. He had walked the earth for over two thousand years, never knowing death. He had wished for an end to his sentence on earth and only lived to see the end of his purgatory. Samjaya made it his practice not to see or speak to angels or demons but keep to himself.

As Samjaya sat at the table, he said, "Not many of you fuckers"—watchers—"left, are there?"

Lilith said, "What do you mean? You are one of us fuckers, asshole."

Samjaya felt like his sentence to walk the earth mostly wasn't his fault and resented the remaining, especially Lilith and Azazel.

Lucifer said, "Now, Sam, don't you want this shit to be over? Help us, and we'll help you."

Samjaya—Sam, as Lucifer called him—asked, "How and why does the devil need my help?"

Lucifer said that there was a descendant of Moses that was interfering with their plans and he needed to be dealt with.

Sam said, "There have been others. Why not just kill him?"

Lucifer said, "These two have tried at least twice and failed. Something is different with this one. Until all the descendants of light are killed or corrupted, the end of days can't begin."

So it was in Samjaya's best interest to assist them. Samjaya asked what Lucifer needed him to do.

Lucifer said that he wanted Samjaya to do what his original mandate from God entailed. "Watch Sonny."

Lucifer told Samjaya to make Sonny's life more difficult than it already was. Lucifer told Sam that Azazel and Lilith were going to make him estranged from his family via Anne, and then when he's good and alone, she would leave him.

Lucifer said, "If we can't kill him, we'll neuter him."

Lucifer's vessel (the teenage girl) began to turn gray, and her veins became more vascular. Her body was failing. No human walked in by Lucifer could survive for very long. Lucifer leaned against the window/wall of the café as Azazel took the ball cap off her head and tilted it to cover her eyes as they closed and the red glow of Lucifer faded. The three remaining—Azazel, Lilith, and Samjaya—got up from the table and left the café, walking in different directions.

Sonny was working swing shift as the Burbank bicycle sergeant of the downtown city-walk district. There were a lot of shops, restaurants, and bars; and it was definitely busy with foot traffic, intoxicated people, and fights. He usually had about six to eight officers on his team, and they were fast and in shape. They would ride in single-line formation like a mobile SWAT team. They would ride up fast, encircle a problem, and handle it. Sonny trained his officers how to enter fast, dismount the bikes, and control violent people with poetic efficiency. Sonny's martial art and defensive tactics experience came in useful for this assignment. It was fun and challenging. For the most part, the officers that worked on his team were high-energy guys that understood his methodology. Some military units refer to this type of unit as a "fire team," and Sonny ran it that way. They worked hard when they needed to, but he made sure they got their downtime to decompress also. Often Sonny would have coffee with them as a team, so they got comfortable around him in nonstress situations so that they would not act differently when he was around for hot calls. Sonny had a lot of fun as a bike sergeant, and he enjoyed going to work. It was a nice change for him after all he had been through.

Sonny was a by-the-book kind of supervisor. He wouldn't engage in any activity that he or his officers would have to look over his shoulder for. There was another bike team with opposite days off that had a different philosophy. Instead of probable cause, they believed in probable cause. So neither the sergeants nor the officers saw eye to eye.

Luke was about four, and Joshua was two years old. Anne was working as a part-time cosmetologist, and the boys went to a local day care during the day while she worked. Sonny's anxiety had recessed, and he was positive and doing okay. He was walking into a diner for his lunch break with Sergeant Tinsley when he got a call from Anne. She was on her way to the ER with Joshua, who had a temperature of 104. Sonny called his lieutenant and said that he had to go home sick and explained the situation. Sonny rode back to the precinct in panic mode, got changed, and headed to the hospital. When he arrived, Joshua was burning up and had not been seen by a doctor. Instead of the traditional triage philosophy, the ER staff was taking everyone in order. As staff took a grossly intoxicated adult into a back room, Sonny's blood began to boil. He was holding his two-year-old in his arms as he helplessly watched others get to see a doctor first. It had been almost two hours since Joshua arrived and got checked in. Sonny yelled to a nurse as she walked by.

Sonny said, "My son has a 104-degree fever, and you're taking drunks first? At what point does this become a medical emergency?"

She replied, "Oh, it's an emergency right now. He could go into a fatal seizure right now."

Sonny said, "Then why in the fuck am I still sitting in your lobby?"

She looked over at the charge nurses' station, and there was no one there, just a man who had been at the computer walking away from the desk. He was in scrubs, but his face was not familiar to the nurse Sonny was talking to. She quickly walked to the desk where everyone in the lobby was placed in order of priority and came back to Sonny seconds later. She told Sonny that she did not know how this happened but his son kept being placed at the bottom of the list. Hospital staff moved quickly and took Joshua to a room where he was immediately placed in a bath and given ibuprofen. His fever came down shortly thereafter.

But who was the man at the charge nurses' desk? It was Samjaya. He had begun the devil's work, but he was conflicted. He knew it was wrong, but he wanted the endlessness of his existence to end. He exited the hospital out a back door to a parking lot that was dimly lit and where out-of-service ambulances were parked. As he walked from the door, he was spun around violently by a man that had him by the shoulder. The man's other arm was up against Samjaya's throat. Remember that Samjaya is six feet, four inches, and strong. This man was considerably shorter, maybe five feet, ten inches. The unknown man took off his hood and revealed his face to Samjaya. It was whom Sonny knew as Father Joel, but his real identity is the archangel Johel.

Samjaya sarcastically said, "Hello, Johel, it's been a long time."

While pressing his forearm against Samjaya's throat, Archangel Johel was *pissed*!

Archangel Johel said, "You almost fucking killed that kid. You picked the wrong side once. Don't do it again."

Samjaya told Archangel Johel that his sentence by their Father was unjust and he wanted it to end. He didn't fornicate with humans as the other watchers did, but Lucifer was his brother. By now, Archangel Johel had released his forearm from Samjaya's throat, and the two stood and spoke to each other. Archangel Johel told Samjaya that Lucifer had changed. He was jealous and greedy then, and the last two thousand years have made him worse. Archangel Johel told him that he might not be able to die, but if he pulled another stunt like that, Archangel Johel would drop him in a box in the Atlantic Ocean for the rest of eternity.

Sanjaya asked, "What's so special about Sonny? Why is he different than any other descendant of light?"

Archangel Johel did not answer the question. He told Sanjaya, "Before this is over, you'll have to make a choice. Make the right one."

Archangel Johel revealed his wings for a second that enveloped him in a golden light. His figure constricted like a fission bomb into a sphere of light that was floating about chest high and then disappeared. Samjaya's body sank as if weakened from exhaustion as he exclaimed fuck under his breath. Contact with an angel weakens the human body, even for Samjaya.

Back inside the hospital, Joshua's fever had broken, and Sonny and Anne sat quietly in a room with him. They thought they were alone, but Lilith was there prepared to follow Lucifer's instructions.

Anne broke the silence by saying, "You didn't have to snap on that nurse," Lilith's words through Anne's voice.

Sonny was defensive and asked what she was talking about. Anne referred the ER nurse whom Sonny raised his voice to, to get Joshua in a room. Sonny asked Anne if she noticed that their son was burning up and they were taking drunks before their baby. Needless to say, this whisper from Lilith sparked an argument that caused tension throughout the rest of the day. Mission accomplished so far.

Back in the highest level of heaven, archangels Michael, Gabriel, Uriel, and Johel met to discuss the watchers increasing their harassment of Sonny and now his sons. They were in their true angelic forms. Michael, Gabriel, and Uriel were tall with huge beautiful wings. Johel was shorter, but his wings were just as big and bright. They sat at a white table with circular benches. It appeared like what one would expect from King Arthur's round table but white and beautiful. Around them were giant marble stones like Stonehenge, surrounded by clouds like a floating island.

Johel started by asking, "Where is Raphael?"

Michael said, "He was checking in on another issue."

Archangel Uriel, never short on the ability to be blunt, said sarcastically, "Oh yeah? What's that?"

Gabriel said, "The soul of a descendant of Miriam [Moses' sister] was about to leave the Guf and be born into the human world. Another descendant of light was entering the world, and Raphael was there to bear witness."

Archangel Michael brought the group back to the focus of their assembly and demanded a report. Archangel Johel said they had a new problem. The cursed one, the walker of eternity, had joined the side of evil. Johel said Samjaya was actively assisting Lucifer and explained what happened at the hospital. Archangel Johel told the group that he appeared to Sam and threatened him to stay out of it. Archangel Johel said Samjaya wanted to know why heaven was protecting Sonny so much and what was so special about this descendant of light.

Archangel Michael said, "It is not for them to know that Sonny is the seventieth son of the seventieth son."

Long ago, there was a prophecy that the corruption of the seventieth son of the seventieth son was a step toward the Apocalypse. Archangel Michael told the group it was time for one of them to appear to Sonny, not in a dream and not in human form, but in their true angelic appearance. Archangel Gabriel said that he would do it.

Archangel Michael said, "Your appearance is startling to any human you have ever shown yourself to. You even scare me. No, not you. Sorry."

Archangel Uriel said that he would do it. Archangel Michael sarcastically said that Uriel was skilled at dispensing justice to demons, watchers, and sinners; his personal skills with communication weren't his strong point.

Gabriel said, "You mean he's an asshole?"

Archangel Uriel shrugged and motioned his hands upward with palms up that he conceded that he was an asshole. Archangel Michael told Johel that it had to be him. Sonny knew Archangel Johel as Father Joel, and he could start with that and explain the truth. Then he could reveal his true identity. It was time for Sonny to know.

Archangel Michael said, "As for Samjaya…"

Michael said Samjaya was a reluctant participant in the rebellion. He was confused then, and now he just wanted his punishment to be over. Michael told the group to monitor Samjaya but try not to contact him unless he was going to do something harmful to Sonny or his family. Archangel Michael said that Samjaya's role in this was yet to unfold completely.

Sonny was working about a week later. He was riding his mountain bike downtown with one of his officers. He was stopped at a light waiting at a crosswalk. The light turned green, and he started riding, clipping his feet in the pedals. The driver of a southbound SUV had spilled his drink in his lap, and he was distracted, no doubt from a little help from Azazel who had flicked the cup from his hand at a well-timed bump in the road. He plowed right through the red light, running over Sonny in the process. Sonny's duty belt became lodged in the front bumper upon contact, which prevented him from being completely run over. The bicycle went under the SUV and was completely mangled. The vehicle came to a sudden stop halfway through the intersection, and Sonny fell to the ground. The officer that was with Sonny saw the whole thing and radioed for an ambulance. Sonny looked like he'd been hit by a car. He was wearing a white polo shirt that bike cops wear and blue utility pants. His clothing was filthy, and police equipment was on the ground everywhere. The radio, pepper spray, gun magazines, keys, etc. looked like they were thrown in the intersection. Sonny said he felt okay, but the shift lieutenant came to the scene and insisted that Sonny go to a hospital and be checked out.

Sonny was black and blue from his hip to his ankle. After a few MRIs and an examination, the ER doctor told Sonny that he was going to be sore as hell, but nothing was broken. The ER doctor was amazed. There was a nurse that was particularly nice to Sonny. A tall brunette named Simone had been wheeling him to different rooms for MRIs, blood work, etc. They struck up a conversation throughout his visit, and they flirted a little. Simone had a high IQ, and she was very quick witted, snarky like Sonny. They got along great. Simone was the opposite of Sonny's wife. She was caring and complementary to Sonny.

At one point, she entered his room saying, "Hey, handsome, how's the leg?"

Sonny wasn't used to getting compliments. It was nice to have an attractive woman be nice to him, and he forgot about the pain his body was feeling. Once it was determined that Sonny didn't have to stay the night, Simone said goodbye and she would go take care of his discharge papers from the discharge nurse. A few minutes later, a man dressed as a nurse in scrubs backed his way into the room with papers in his hand as he said thank you to Simone.

He was about five feet, ten inches, and had dark hair and a medium build—looked like an average guy. He closed the door and the blinds and then turned around. When Sonny saw his face, his stomach sank. It was Father Joel. Sonny's expression reflected the confusion he was feeling. There was an awkward moment of silence.

Then Archangel Johel said, "I can explain. You know me as Father Joel, but I am the archangel Johel. It's time you know the truth of your bloodline."

Sonny replied, "Bullshit."

Archangel Johel's wings burst open and extended around the inside of the hospital room. Each feather glistened with a golden glow. They were absolutely magnificent. Sonny sat in shock. But he had similar visuals in his dreams, so he remained rational. Archangel Johel retracted his wings and sat down in a chair by the hospital bed that Sonny was sitting on.

Archangel Johel reminded Sonny about the meeting where he explained that the battle for humanity wasn't fought in the sky, with Lucifer transforming into a dragon to be slain by Archangel Michael with a flaming sword. Lucifer attempted to corrupt human souls daily and generally Angels didn't directly interfere with humans' free will. Archangel Johel told Sonny that, at any given time, there were what they call descendants of light on earth that were here to tip the scales.

Sonny asked, "What is a descendant of light?"

Archangel Johel told Sonny that, throughout time, there had been people that were touched by the power of God, such as Moses. The descendants/bloodline of these people had been bestowed with divine gifts. Some of these descendants had a more profound connection with the gift. Some chalked it up to intuition and never really realized their potential.

Sonny asked Archangel Johel, "What does that have to do with me?"

Archangel Johel told him that he already knew this, but he was a descendant of the great prophet Moses.

Sonny said, "And what is it that I am required to do because of this?"

Johel said, "Not just what you are required to do, but what you could do."

The watchers saw him as a threat, and they would never stop harassing and trying to corrupt him.

Sonny asked, "Watchers? What are they?"

Archangel Johel explained that the watchers were a group of about two hundred angels tasked with watching mankind but never interfering. Led by Lucifer, his top lieutenants were Azazel, Lilith, and Samjaya. The watchers disobeyed God and lay with mortal women, producing children. God ordered the children (Nephilim) to be put down, and most were. The remaining few were trapped in hell. Archangel Johel told Sonny that Samjaya was the only watcher not to lie with women and produce offspring, but he did side with his friend Lucifer in the rebellion. So as punishment, he was not sent to hell and deformed like the others. He was sentenced to walk the earth, never knowing a mortal death but knowing mortal suffering.

Archangel Johel told Sonny, "Samjaya is not a neutral participant. He still aligns with Lucifer. Watch out for him."

Archangel Johel told Sonny that, when a descendant of light was born, it was like a beacon of light shining in the sky, and Moses was kind of a big deal. Archangel Johel asked Sonny if he knew what happened to him when he was five years old and he was a victim of a SIDS death but brought back with CPR. Sonny vaguely knew his own story of that incident from what his older sister, Marcy, had told him. Archangel Johel told him that he was actually killed by the watcher demon Azazel. Azazel reached into his heart and squeezed it until it stopped, but it wasn't the CPR that saved him.

Sonny was a little shocked and asked, "But how then?"

Archangel Johel said, "This part gets a little complicated, and it is rarely ever done because it borders on God's rule of noninterference."

Archangel Johel asked Sonny when was the last time he was sick. It had been so long that he couldn't remember. Archangel Johel asked Sonny, other than the stabbing that missed his aorta, if he had ever broken a bone or been seriously injured.

Sonny said, "Take a look around. I'm in a hospital after being hit by a car."

Archangel Johel rhetorically said, "Yeah, anything broken? You became incarnate with an angel to save your life."

Sonny asked, "Are you telling me there is an angel in my head?"

Archangel Johel said, "Imagine you're the driver of a car. There is a passenger in the car, but he's not in control of it. You can call it intuition or a spiritual nudge, but that's how he communicates with you, but he doesn't make decisions for you."

Sonny asked, "Well, what's his name?"

"His name is Raguel, but his friends call him Rags."

Sonny asked, "Why hasn't he left?"

Sonny was alive and aware of all this now. Archangel Johel told Sonny that Rags was along for the whole ride—until Sonny died.

Sonny said, "Wow, that's one serious commitment."

Archangel Johel told Sonny that a human life span was a blink of an eye to an angel and, besides that, Rags was keeping Sonny alive. If Rags abandons ship now, Sonny would die.

Sonny sarcastically asked, "Any other reason I was saved?"

Archangel Johel told him that there was a prophecy of the corruption of the seventieth son of the seventieth son being a part of the end of days.

Sonny asked, "Let me guess. That's me."

Johel, "Yep."

Sonny replied, "Great, I'm one of the signs of the freaking apocalypse."

Johel told Sonny that there was good news, though, regarding that prophecy.

Sonny asked, "What's that?"

Johel explained that, if Sonny was not corrupted or killed by his forty-third birthday, then the prophecy of the seventieth son of the seventieth son would go unfulfilled.

Meanwhile, in the hallway just outside of the room, an orderly was standing just outside of the room. He began to turn gray, and his face became vascular. His eyes were glowing red just like the girl from the diner that was possessed by Lucifer. Well, guess what? So was he. But his body was breaking down, and Lucifer had heard enough anyway. His eyes returned to normal as he collapsed. There were other nurses that saw him sink to the floor, and they came to his aid. None of this was seen by Archangel Johel or Sonny because the blinds were shut and the door was closed. The damage was done. Lucifer got the answers he was looking for.

Sonny asked Archangel Johel, "Where do we go from here?"

Archangel Johel asked Sonny if he had ever heard of Joshua from the Bible.

Sonny said, "You mean the guy that took over for Moses after he delivered the Ten Commandments and died shortly thereafter?"

Archangel Johel replied, "Yeah, that guy."

Johel told Sonny that Joshua was also a descendant of light of the bloodline of Noah. Joshua fought for God, saving other descendants of light and vanquishing demon watchers. Archangel Johel told Sonny that Joshua killed almost fifty watchers during his lifetime before his work was done. It was written in the Bible that Joshua knew only combat and war for forty years, so it became impossible for him to distinguish friend from foe. One day, on the eve of battle, a man appeared on a road; and Joshua charged at him with his sword drawn, demanding to know if the man was an ally or an enemy. As he drew closer, he discovered that the man was the archangel Gabriel. Archangel Gabriel told Joshua that he was neither friend nor foe. It was then that Joshua was freed from his commitment.

Sonny asked Archangel Johel, "What does that have to do with me?"

Archangel Johel told Sonny that he was going to be required to perform similar duties to that of Joshua. Archangel Johel explained that the watchers tried to kill descendants of light at birth—in Sonny's case, as toddlers—

and sometimes they tried to corrupt DOLs (descendants of light) if they made it to adulthood.

Sonny said, "And?"

Archangel Johel told Sonny that he would be required to defend DOLs from being killed by a watcher, or it could be as simple as not letting a DOL drive drunk from a bar.

Sonny asked, "Is there that many DOLs in the LA area?"

Archangel Johel told Sonny this would take him all over the world. It would be case-by-case tasks.

Sonny said he had a life, a wife, and kids and he was a police officer. How was he supposed to travel around the world fighting demons and saving people?

Archangel Johel told Sonny, "I'll take care of the travel arrangements."

Archangel Johel's wings burst open again, covering the room, and it was evident that he was about to leave.

Sonny said, "Hey, I have a thousand more questions."

Archangel Johel's wings enveloped him, concealing his body. He constricted into a ball of energy that hovered and disappeared just like when Archangel Uriel vanished after visiting Sonny in the hospital after he was stabbed. Sonny sank into the hospital bed and was very fatigued. He just had an elongated contact with an angel, and that takes something out of a person, even Sonny. Sonny was released from the hospital, and Sergeant Brentavious Tinsley gave him a ride back to the station where his car was parked. There wasn't much conversation, and Brentavious just chalked it up to Sonny having a long day. But Sonny was processing everything that just happened and was still kind of in shock. How does he fight a demon? How could he protect his family from this? Who was this Samjaya guy, and was he sneaking around? These were his own thoughts, even his own, or were they Raguel's?

His thoughts crashed in his head like an unanchored boat on a rough sea. He went into the station and got changed out of his uniform in the locker room. As he was washing his face, trying to clear his head, he caught a glimpse of himself in the mirror and felt a little dysphoric.

He looked into his own eyes and said aloud, "Raguel, are you there?"

Nothing happened, except an officer walking by that Sonny hadn't noticed. His name was Andy and asked if Sonny was okay. Sonny awoke from his inner thoughts and replied that he was and that he was just thinking.

Lucifer did use the body of the orderly to listen in on the conversation that Sonny had with Archangel Johel, but he didn't hear the whole thing. The orderly's body was breaking down, so he vacated before Archangel Johel told Sonny what was going to be asked of him in the future. But Lucifer heard enough. He'd lived up to his end of the bargain at the diner when he was giving Azazel, Lilith, and Samjaya their marching orders. It was time to speak to them again.

Azazel, Lilith, and Samjaya arrived at the same diner early one morning a few days after Sonny was hit by the car. They waited and watched the door to the diner for Lucifer's arrival. A younger, teenage Black male came through the door. He had a backpack slung over his shoulder and a letterman jacket on. He was a big kid, like a football player, except this football player had eyes of fire and looked pissed. He approached the table and again asked if he could join them and motioned to sit down next to Samjaya. Lilith and Azazel were seated next to each other. Samjaya was irritated and said he had begun interfering with Sonny's life but asked why they were meeting so soon again. Lucifer asked Samjaya what he had done to Sonny. Samjaya told the group what he had done to Sonny's son Joshua at the ER but got a little visit after from the angel Johel.

Azazel said, "You had direct contact with an angel?"

Samjaya replied, "You could say that. He choked the shit out of me, threatened me, and then did the flashy angel disappear thing."

Angels had a pretty strict hands-off policy regarding interfering with humanity.

Azazel asked aloud of the group, "What the hell is with this guy Sonny?"

Lucifer said to the group, "Not only is Sonny a descendant of Moses. Sonny is the seventieth son of the seventieth son and has a part to play at the end of days if we can kill or corrupt him before his forty-third birthday."

Azazel said aloud to the group, "Sonny is uncommonly resilient."

Lilith asked if this was how he survived when Azazel killed Sonny at five years old. Lucifer told the group that the angel Raguel was incarnate with Sonny to keep him alive.

Lilith asked, "Is there any way to break the incarnation?"

Lucifer said, "Short of a good, old-fashioned voluntary exorcism, no."

Azazel said, "Maybe we can make Sonny want to get rid of Raguel?"

Lucifer replied, "Not likely. He is aware that, without Raguel, he would die."

Samjaya, who had been quiet so far, asked the group, "Then what? What now? If this guy is so important to them, what now? You three are immortals without the fear of pain. I feel all that shit, and the angels are pissed."

Azazel told Samjaya, "Worried about your ass, huh, Sam?"

Sam replied, "Damn right I am."

Lucifer said to the group that they would test this Sonny and see what he was capable of. Lucifer told the group he had a hunch that Sonny's use to God may have gone beyond dreams and minimal intervention. Azazel asked what he had in mind. Lucifer asked the group if they knew of any descendants of light that were young and sure to be protected. Lilith told the group that a daughter of Miriam was recently born in London and must be important because the archangel Raphael was there to witness the birth.

Lucifer told the group to make it look like a home invasion or burglary, but they would go after the baby to draw out the angels' plans. Lucifer told Azazel that he wanted the demons Turiel and Zaqiel to walk into two men who were extremely violent and had long criminal records so that the attack would not be questioned.

Azazel asked Lucifer, "Why not have me and Lilith do it?"

Lucifer told them, if his hunch was right, they'd be glad it wasn't them. Lucifer told them, "In chess, the pawns go first."

Samjaya asked what was he to do. Lucifer told him that he was on the angels' radar and to back off for now. If the angels saw Samjaya, the plan would be telegraphed too much. That was a relief for Samjaya because he had mixed feelings although his face did not reveal his apprehension. Azazel asked when Lucifer wanted this to happen.

Lucifer said, "Give it about six months to a year, earth time. Let Sonny settle into normalcy and allow any vigilance to subside."

About then, the body Lucifer was inhabiting began to break down as the others did. Lucifer vacated, and the young football player found himself exhausted but conscious at a table with three strangers. He was in shock as they got up and walked out without saying a word.

In the following months, Sonny's life had settled a bit. He had a prophetic dream here and there, but nothing major had happened. He went to work and handled calls for service and supervised his team. Things were okay with his wife, which basically meant no major fights. Luke and Joshua were okay and were about three and five years old at that time. It was a swing shift at about 11:00 p.m.; a call came out for a burglary alarm at Holy Cross Church. This was where he first met Father Joel, a.k.a. Angel Johel. Sonny got a nudge that he should take that call. He got on the radio and told dispatch that he would handle that call and advised on a cover unit. He parked just out of sight from the church and approached on foot. All of the lights were off, and there was no activity. Sonny saw that the door to the main hall was ajar and took his flashlight out and entered the building. As he made his way past pews toward the altar in the center aisle, a bright light appeared behind him, casting his shadow to the altar. He turned around and saw a bright light that began to fade and revealed the figure of a man. It was the angel Johel standing behind him with his wings glowing brightly.

Johel retracted his wings and said, "Let's talk."

Archangel Johel told Sonny that there was a threat to a descendant of light.

Sonny asked, "Who and where?"

Archangel Johel explained that it was a child in England, about a year old, a descendant of Moses's sister, Miriam, so kind of like his cousin. Sonny said that he was aware that the information was coming from an angel, but the cop instinct in him prompted him to ask how Johel knew this. Johel told Sonny that all angels served different purposes and seeing the future was one of Archangel Gabriel's greatest powers. Sonny asked if he would ever meet Archangel Gabriel. Johel told Sonny that Gabriel was almost pure light and emitted peace, but his appearance could be quite jarring to humans. So better that Johel delivered the information for now. Sonny asked Johel what the threat was. Johel explained that watchers were going to attempt to kill the child and Sonny was going to stop them. Sonny asked Johel how he was supposed to do that.

Johel replied, "You're a cop. You have a gun, a night-stick, and heck, you even have pepper spray?"

Sonny said that London, England, was a little out of his jurisdiction.

Johel told Sonny, "Don't worry about that," as he revealed his wings; and they wrapped around both of them.

His wings began to constrict and glow brightly. They transformed into two spheres of light and disappeared.

A blink of an eye later, they reappeared in a large park at about 5:00 a.m. in Saint John, New Brunswick, between Nova Scotia and Maine. It was dark and cloudy and had just rained. They were across the street from what Sonny saw as narrow townhomes with the park at their backs. There were a lot of trees spaced out along the street, and it looked like a pleasant neighborhood. There were cars parked tightly in front of the houses, and each townhome was painted a different light-pastel color. Johel and Sonny were standing next to each other but behind a tree so as not to be very visible to any pedestrians in the area. (There were only a couple of scattered people walking their dogs in the park anyway.) Johel pointed at a lavender-colored home and directed Sonny's attention to it.

Johel said, "Do you see that one? The baby Josephine is about to get a visit from demon watchers. Don't let them kill her. Good luck."

Johel disappeared. He didn't leave with the usual pomp and circumstance, no burst of bright light and vanishing sphere thing. He just vanished.

Sonny thought to himself, *How am I supposed to do this?*

Sonny was in his LA Police uniform in a foreign country about to confront demons in an attempt to stop them from killing a baby, and the angel that brought him there just disappeared. Oh, and he couldn't be killed or corrupted before his forty-third birthday, or the end of days would be triggered.

He thought to himself, *Shouldn't I have some kind of special angel weapon for this?*

His heart was racing as the realization of the moment began to hit him. He gathered himself and started to do some combat breathing: four seconds deep breath in, hold for four seconds, and exhale for four seconds. Rinse and repeat until the heart rate slows. He had been doing this since he was a child to try to get to sleep when demons would haunt his dreams. Sonny had been doing it for his whole life to anchor himself in the present.

As his heart rate slowed, he thought, *Wait a minute. I've been preparing for this my entire life, physically and spiritually.*

He realized that the angel Raguel was with him and he wasn't alone. It was not like he had never been in a fight. He was a black belt and had been in the ring hundreds of times. A strange calm overcame him.

Sonny's attention was drawn to a vehicle's headlights turning off as it was entering the area. Strange because it wasn't parked. It was continuing on the street toward the house with the lights off. The car parked a few houses away from the lavender-colored house that Archangel Johel pointed out. Sonny's eyes, normally a green/hazel, turned into pearls of sky blue. Just then, Sonny saw a pale-blue faint glow appear around his hands. He looked down with curiosity as it continued to flow around his forearms and then his whole body. Like a spiritual armor, he knew it was from Raguel.

Sonny thought, *Here we go. Save the kid. Don't die!*

Two men exited the car. Sonny could see their red demon glow and knew this was it. They started to walk toward the house. One was tall—about six feet, five inches—and made of muscle: Turiel. He looked like an NBA power forward. The other guy was about Sonny's size—six feet, two inches—and athletic: Zaqiel. They were both dressed in dark clothes and were walking quickly but not jogging or running. He couldn't make out their faces, but the red glows kind of gave them away. As they approached, Sonny's police instincts kicked in. He stepped away from his concealed position and revealed himself to the two demons.

Sonny shouted, "Police! Don't move!" as he drew his sidearm and pointed it at them. His voice reverberated like two speakers that weren't quite synchronized. The demons stopped, turned toward Sonny, and smiled. They started to walk toward Sonny.

Turiel said, "An LA cop in Canada? What are you going to do, shoot us?"

Sonny ordered them to stop, which they did about ten feet away. The demons had a point. They hadn't shown any weapons, and Sonny was a little out of his jurisdiction. So he holstered his sidearm. Was this going just be a conversation or a fight?

Zaqiel said, "Let us not play games or mince words, son of Moses."

Sonny replied, "You know me? Who are you?"

Turiel told Sonny that who they were wasn't important. What was important was that Sonny was not going to live to see his forty-third birthday. Turiel and Zaqiel started sidestepping away from each other as they spoke until Sonny had been triangulated and had to split his vision and attention on both demons. There was a brief moment of silence while the three sized each other up, and now Sonny knew an attack was imminent.

He sarcastically said, "What, no more small talk?" to give himself an extra second to visualize his defensive plan.

Sonny had to put himself in high-speed thought, and he had to think tactically if he had a shot of winning this fight. He quickly pivoted in a semicircle, like a boxer. So he wasn't triangulated anymore, and his two opponents were lined up. This meant that he could basically fight one at a time as Turiel and Zaqiel had to go around one another to get to Sonny.

He circled to Turiel's side because he was the larger of the two and he wanted to engage him first. Sonny figured that Turiel was larger but possibly slower. Sonny was no small guy and was extremely athletic, but with Raguel's active assistance, Sonny was faster and stronger than he'd ever known. The two demons were lined up in a flash. A celestial fist to cuffs was on with red and blue glowing auras shining in the early-morning dawn. Turiel took a big swing with his right at Sonny's head. Sonny took a half step back, and Turiel missed by a mile. After the punch went by and before Turiel could reset, Sonny hit Turiel on the left side of his face with a straight right that spun Turiel around like a top and dropped him right there. Turiel looked like a fall victim. Turiel's spirit left the body of the man he had inhabited and disappeared, fading into the ground. Sonny didn't stop to admire his work. He stepped over Turiel and advanced on Zaqiel. Zaqiel was in shock. Sonny was advancing on him, with his eyes beaming with blue light and his fists clenched. Zaqiel turned and ran toward the car that he had arrived in. Sonny gave chase for ten to fifteen feet and then stopped as Zaqiel got in the car and began to put the car in reverse and slam on the gas pedal. Sonny turned and walked back to where Turiel was knocked out.

Turiel had regained consciousness and was slowly trying to get to all fours. It wasn't Turiel anymore. The guy was a lifetime criminal named Stockwell and muscle for organized crime hiding out in Quebec to avoid prosecution for several murders in the United States. Stockwell was dazed and confused. He looked up and saw Sonny in his LAPD uniform and asked if Sonny was there to take him back to LA. Sonny knew that this guy was being used by Turiel but deserved what he got. Sonny told him to get the fuck out of there and stay out of the USA. Stockwell stumbled away on foot. Sonny stood there for a second with his hands on his hips, proud of himself for what had just happened. His eyes returned to hazel, and the baby-blue aura dissipated away. His attention was drawn to movement on his right, then he looked and saw Johel standing next to him.

Sonny said, "Thanks for the help. You take off just when the fun was about to start."

Johel replied, "I had faith that you and Rags had it covered. Besides, I wasn't gone. I just chose not to be visible."

Sonny asked, "Now what the hell does that mean?"

Johel replied, "It means you passed this test."

Sonny was irritated at that statement and said with a raised voice, "Why are you testing me?"

To that, Johel replied that it wasn't he that was testing Sonny. Archangel Johel opened his wings, and they enveloped the two. With a burst of light, they were reduced to spheres of energy and disappeared. They reappeared instantly at the church, and no time had passed. The police dispatcher asked Sonny over the radio if he was code 4. After all, he did respond to a call for service of a burglary at that location.

Sonny took out his radio and answered, "No further assistance needed," while maintaining eye contact with Johel.

Johel disappeared in his usual flashy style. Sonny returned to his patrol car and went back to work, reliving the incident over and over again in his mind, how to reconcile the fact that he was just teleported by an angel twice, never mind the fact that he was just in a fight with demons. He wondered how Joshua felt after the first time he had fought for God. He was also asking himself if he had to be God's soldier for forty years like Joshua was before he could be released from service. Sonny was also aware that the watchers' attacks would not subside, especially before he was forty-three years old.

Meanwhile, in the park in Saint John, New Brunswick, an elderly man stood in the park near where the fight between good and evil had just taken place, walking two Yorkshire terriers. He was hardly noticeable in the grand scheme of things, except this man had eyes of fire, and the two dogs transformed into Azazel and Lilith. They had witnessed Sonny in action and were concerned. Johel was right. It wasn't his test; it was Lucifer's. Sonny was going to be a real challenge for them.

Lucifer said, "As I said, the pawns go first."

Azazel replied, "He won't be corrupted, especially now that Raguel is active."

Lucifer said they would have to kill Sonny. Lucifer told Azazel and Lilith to keep after him. He was a police officer, so they would have plenty of opportunities. Sonny was about thirty-five years old at that time, so they had about eight years to get the job done. The next five years of Sonny's life would not see many peaceful moments.

Sonny was always in the action at work. He enjoyed the fast-paced excitement of his assignment as a bike sergeant. The watchers took full advantage of Sonny's occupation, and the attacks and attempts on Sonny's life happened frequently. He didn't talk to his wife, Anne, a lot about work and certainly not about the supernatural turn his life had taken. She would continue to hear knocks and strange noises in the house. She and the boys would catch an occasional shadow or strange light as well, but the watchers weren't focused on her or the kids at this time.

Sonny loved dogs and always had at least one, sometimes two. At this point in his life, the family dog was a three-year-old Australian shepherd named Choyo, who was about to be joined by an English black Lab. His name was Smokey, and he was built like a Rottweiler. Smokey had a huge block head and was super loving. Sonny, Joshua, and

Luke were visiting the local animal shelter one day; and Smokey had caught their attention. He was like a bear. He would come to the fence door and stand up on his hind legs and hold their hands like he was trying to hug them. It was weird, almost like there was a sentient being inside him. Sonny noticed that there was a purple sticker on his informational paper that was displayed on the top of his pen. Sonny asked one of the employees what the sticker meant because they were thinking about adopting him. The employee told Sonny and the boys, who were about three and five at this time, that the sticker meant that the dog was scheduled to be put down.

Sonny told the employee that they were going to think about it but asked how much time they had.

She replied, "Don't think too long. He's getting put down today after the close of business."

That was enough for Sonny.

He said, "We'll take him."

They ran home and got Choyo to bring him back to the pound to do the doggy meet and greet to make sure the two would get along. It was a requirement by the animal shelter before Smokey could be released to them. They broke the news to Anne that they wanted to get another dog. Initially she was not happy, but that was no big shock. She agreed to go to the pound anyway with them and Choyo for the doggy compatibility test. They waited in a small grassy courtyard for the two dogs to meet. Choyo was a medium-sized dog with one blue eye and one brown eye. He was a great dog but was alone a lot at the house. Sonny and the boys felt like he needed a buddy, and this was how they sold it to Anne. He generally got along with other dogs, but he was a scrapper. Choyo weighed about seventy pounds.

A couple of the shelter volunteers retrieved Smokey from his pen and opened the door to the courtyard. This was a moment. Sonny felt like he did when he was about to fight Turiel and Zaqiel. Luke and Joshua really wanted Smokey, and this was Smokey's last chance. As the volunteers walked Smokey in the courtyard and he looked around surveying the scene, it was eerie. Smokey was about 120 pounds, all black with dark-brown eyes. He was even bigger than he looked in his pen. His head was down, but his eyes were up. Sonny walked Choyo over to Smokey for the big test. There was a brief moment of nonmovement and silence as Sonny's family and the shelter staff watched and waited with bated breath. Then suddenly the two dogs started wagging their tails and licking each other's faces like they were long-lost friends.

A couple of minutes later, they were running around the courtyard playing. Smokey had a new home, saved on his last day. It didn't take long for Smokey to acclimate to the house either. He fit right in, but he also saw more than Choyo. Choyo either didn't see or ignored the spirits that were always around, but either way, he didn't often display behaviors that he was seeing them. Smokey, on the other hand, was different. Smokey bonded with the boys almost immediately, and he was uncommonly protective of them. Sonny and Anne lived in a medium-sized single-story home. There was a long hallway in the house leading to the boys' bedrooms and the master bedroom. Smokey would often sit at the entrance to that hallway and growl toward the end of it, but nothing was there. He would also often put his head down and stalk an invisible something at the end of the hall. Whatever it was, Smokey didn't like it.

The boys' bedrooms were directly across from each other, and Smokey would sleep in between the two doors like a Roman centurion guarding a post. Anne was fully convinced that the house was haunted. Sonny didn't confide in her about his incarnate angel or the fact that it was he that was haunted, not the house. Sonny felt better about going to work and leaving the boys home with Anne with Smokey around, not just for any supernatural disruptions, but also for any possible regular old burglars. Smokey was always vigilant, and that rubbed off on Choyo as well. The two dogs were the guardians of the house when Sonny was not home.

Sonny's marriage was strained to say the least, with all the shift work and late nights. Anne would tell him that the kids were in bed for the night when he was working swing shift, but in actuality, she would have her mom or another sitter come over and watch them while she hit the clubs with her friend Misty. Misty was about Anne's age and wasn't particularly faithful to her husband. The two would go out while Sonny was at work. Her husband was a fireman, so he also had shift work. The two women were basically just biding their time, allowing their husbands' pensions to accumulate until they would take enough in a divorce. Sonny knew it was just a matter of time.

Anne called Sonny one night right before he was about to get off work. Misty had been in a bar fight downtown and fled the area drunk and on foot. Anne asked Sonny to pick her up because Misty's husband couldn't. Sonny obliged because that was what he did for Anne. He acquiesced to try to make her happy. Misty was hammered drunk, and he gave her a ride back to Sonny and Anne's home, where Anne was waiting to take her back to her house. Sonny's marriage was on a slippery slope in addition to what had just happened with Johel. Sonny decided to leave his run-and-gun assignment as a bike sergeant and took a boring job in detectives so he could be home at night and on weekends. It would be better for his marriage but would be more difficult to slip away unnoticed for descendant-of-light assignments.

Sonny put in for the transfer, and it came through quickly. Sonny was wearing a suit and was behind a desk every day working in burglary. Burglary was a thankless job—thousands of reports every week, mostly with no leads whatsoever. Sonny would have to read the cases and assign them if they were workable. There were never enough detectives and a lot of unhappy citizens. Call after call after call was "What are you doing on my case? I've seen *CSI*. Do something!" But this assignment enabled Sonny to be home at night and on weekends, so he thought he might be able to save his marriage. It also allowed him to teach an occasional martial arts class and maybe prepare his sons for what they might have to face in the future. It was important to Sonny that the boys knew how to defend themselves and were free of intimidation, something that Sonny's father wasn't able or willing to do. Sonny's father was shacked up in Reno, and the two didn't talk much.

Burglary was actually good for Sonny. It went on for a couple of years. A routine developed, and so did the boys. At one point, Sonny had his own karate school. He'd started it for his sons but also because he knew what it was like to be small and intimidated. He could relate to kids and people that didn't have a *Brady Bunch* childhood, and he wanted to make a difference. Anne even volunteered to do the books and the billing. Anne had taken tae kwon do as a teen and enjoyed it. She was supportive of the idea. All manners of misfit were drawn to the school. By the time the boys were six and eight, they knew about combat tactics and the psychology of combat more than most adult black belts did, theories of attack timing like recoil, fake, explosion, and movement (Sonny called it his four *A*s of attack). Imagine an eight-year-old understanding the premise of manifesting or self-fulfilling prophecies. The kids understood the concepts of what a person thinks cascades into realities.

It wasn't just Luke and Joshua that were taught these concepts and how to apply them to combat. All the students, eight or eighty and man or woman, got the same knowledge. Sonny had spoken to a couple of therapists in his life. He picked up a few psychology concepts along the way. Between his personal life experiences and some things he picked up from doctors, he was able to teach the mental preparation aspect of combat as well as the physical acts of kicking and punching. Sonny had this routine that the kids would practice before tournaments.

Sonny called it his five-minute anchor. He taught the students to take five minutes to themselves before an athletic competition to get their "heads right." For the first two minutes, the student was supposed to think about the most positive athletic competitive moment in their lives. It could be anything—sparring, basketball, football, track, or whatever. They were supposed to focus on the entirety of the event: the sights, the sounds, the feelings, etc., the whole positive experience. The next two minutes were all about today so that the student can transfer the positive outcome from the past and bring it to today. The student was supposed to visualize defeating the opponents in the room that he or she would possibly face. For two minutes, the student visualized the wins. The last minute was the hardest. The student was supposed to visualize nothingness, eyes closed with no thoughts, just the blackness of inner space.

Sonny felt like the last part of his five-minute anchor was the most important because it slowed the heart rate; and in turn, his students' opponents would be seen as moving in slow motion, almost like Sonny's students were fighting with precognition. It may have been spiritual nudging by Raguel or moments of clarity. Whatever it was, it worked. Sonny's sons and his other students performed and competed with unappalled success. Sonny also competed when time allowed, putting into practice what he taught. It was great for his kids and his students to see him fight. Some instructors don't get in the ring because, if they lose or don't do well, they may be exposed as frauds and revenue could suffer. Sonny wasn't like that. He would hold open-sparring Saturdays for any black belts that wanted to train, not so Sonny could beat them up, but because he believed in inclusion and "the rising tide lifts all boats."

A couple of years after fighting Turiel and Zaqiel were pretty good for Sonny. He settled into a nice routine. His marriage was better, and he was spending time with his sons. The watchers, for whatever reason, left him alone; or so he thought. They had until his forty-third birthday to kill him, and he was almost 38. They had a little over five years to do what they were going to do. Sonny knew he couldn't be corrupted by this point. He was past that. But the watchers weren't done, and Sonny was always aware of that fact. Sonny was a concern for them. But let's face it: they were trying to corrupt mankind, not just Sonny, so they did have other things to do. Well, they got around to it.

Anne's father became ill—terminally ill. She wasn't able to help out at the dojo as much anymore. She spent less and less time there. Sonny was getting burned out also. He would get up at 5:00 a.m. and go to work as a burglary sergeant so that he could get off at 4:00 p.m. He'd go home and walk the dogs and then head to the dojo and teach class until 9:00 p.m. Most days, Anne couldn't be there either. Luke and Joshua were having the time of their lives there though. They always had so much fun. Even though Sonny was stretched thin, he never showed it to the kids or his students. Sonny was always good at putting a positive face on. Plus, teaching gave him a temporary escape from his reality.

Unfortunately it was not possible for Sonny to do all that was required by himself to run a business and have a police career that paid the bills—mortgage payments, car payments, and all the other financial responsibilities that go with being a provider, in addition to being a small-business owner. Anne's part-time cosmetologist career didn't pay much either. Toward the end of the school's existence, there was some positive news though. Sonny was notified that he was going to be inducted into the martial arts hall of fame in a ceremony to be held in his hometown of Buffalo, New York. He thought that it would be a good break and trip for him and Anne.

Sonny's mom watched the boys while Sonny and Anne took the trip. Over the course of the weekend, there were seminars by different famous instructors culminating with a ceremony at the end. It was a great weekend, and Sonny and Anne got to spend some time together. Sonny asked Anne to video his induction speech because this kind of thing only comes once in a lifetime. Sonny got to the podium, as there were various pictures of him in the background from different martial arts events, and gave his speech. He thanked his wife and instructors, etc. He sat after and talked with Anne about how he did and if she got it all on video. Anne told him that she forgot to video. Sonny wasn't happy, but that was her MO. She just wanted to get out of town. She didn't really give a shit about Sonny's recognition. Before they left, she even commented that she didn't even see the big deal about the HOF. Her instructor, when she was a kid, was on the cover of a magazine. Sonny was raised Catholic and got married for life. He wanted his wife to love him, but the truth was that she wouldn't care if he got hit by a bus. Sonny was a means to an end for Anne.

The longer she was married to him, the more she would get of his pension when she would leave him.

Sonny was under a lot of stress. When they returned home, the karate school closed shortly thereafter. He was waiting for this impending doom of his forty-third birthday. His business just closed. He was worried about the boys and what they might face from the watchers as they were descendants of Moses's bloodline as well. His wife treated him like shit, and he was financially strapped. Sonny had a major nocturnal panic attack. At about 3:00 a.m. one day, he awoke with irrational thoughts and fears that were manifested as real possibilities in his mind. He thought he was past this kind of mental challenge but apparently wasn't. The ironic thing was this wasn't pushed by the watchers, so Raguel could not stop it. This came right from Sonny's own subconscious. This was the most terrifying experience of Sonny's life. After all that he had been through, this scary event came from within, which meant that Sonny was his biggest opponent at that time.

He lay in bed while Anne slept, and he was in anguish. He didn't even wake her to talk about it. He just sat there suffering by himself. The next morning, Anne had to go do something with her mother, and Sonny still did not speak of his pain. If only he believed that she would support him, he could tell her. Sonny believed that, if Anne saw him as anything other than the alpha male, she would pounce on him like a lion. He couldn't afford for her to see him as vulnerable. A table's legs will break if enough weight is placed on the table, and Anne wasn't capable of rebuilding him if Sonny admitted he was a little broken. After about a week or two of negative thoughts and anxiety waiting for him any moment his brain wasn't busy, Sonny finally broke down and told Anne.

Anne's reply was "I don't have time for your problems."

Sonny didn't plan to have a life-altering panic attack when Anne's father was on his death bed from cancer, but that was what happened. Sonny was there for Anne as much as he could be but found it difficult to get out of his own head. After a battle with cancer, Anne's father passed away in his sleep. It wasn't a shock. He'd been fighting the illness for a long time. Anne felt like Sonny wasn't there for her as much as he should have. In truth, he was supportive even though the battle for his sanity was raging in his own mind. Anne was angry—angry all the time. Call it mourning, but this was constant. Everyone had to walk on eggshells around Anne. Anne's mom came to live with Sonny and Anne after the passing of Anne's father. Sonny didn't mind that. He loved her mom and was actually nicer to her than Anne was. Anne's father loved Sonny and always appreciated the life that Anne had as a result of her marriage with Sonny, and Sonny loved him too. Anne became more and more resentful of Sonny. For some reason, he had become the villain of her life. Anne always had to have a villain.

Anne discovered a new best friend from her past shortly after that—Pam. Pam lived in Las Vegas, and apparently she and Anne were childhood friends. Anne apparently needed to see "Pam" more and more often. This went on for about a year. Anne returned from one such weekend trip and told Sonny that she needed to talk to him.

They sat in their truck in the parking lot of the salon that Anne worked at, and she told him that she wasn't in love with him anymore. She told him that she would always love him for being a good dad to the boys, but other than that, she was checked out. Anne suggested that they could go to counseling but wasn't sure if anything would change. Azazel and Lilith laughed their watcher asses off. They didn't even have to whisper in anyone's ears for this calamity. It just was. Sonny was thirty-nine. Sonny loved Anne. Even though she took him for granted and dismissed his pain, he still loved her.

Anne agreed to try to work on their marriage but then planned another trip to Las Vegas in February. Sonny was in emotional agony. When she got back from Vegas, he began sleeping on the couch. Sonny was the only one trying, and after that February trip, Sonny stopped trying. The two basically stopped talking to each other, other than a couple of sessions with a marriage counselor. But it was no use. Anne was checked out, and Sonny didn't know what she had done on her trips to Las Vegas or other nightly outings with her friend Misty. The two were separated under the same roof while their house was up for sale. Even though the D-word hadn't been spoken, Sonny knew it was imminent.

Just after his thirty-ninth birthday and three days before Christmas that same year, Anne served Sonny with divorce papers. Sonny was devastated. The house had a buyer. Sonny thought they were going to get a rental together while they rebuilt their finances, but Anne had other plans. She wanted half of the proceeds from the house sale, a kazillion a month of alimony and half his pension—financially outrageous demands. Then she suggested that they use the same divorce lawyer to save money on divorce costs. Holy shit, what a shock. About a month later, the house sold, and their U-Hauls went in different directions. Sonny hired a female divorce lawyer, but she was more interested in her check than helping Sonny. Sonny and Anne sat down with their lawyers to sign the paperwork and discuss how much of his pension she could take. Her lawyer was a tall dark-skinned guy with a beard and mustache. Yep, it was Samjaya. The watchers weren't that far away after all. Samjaya had started getting his hair cut by Anne six months prior in the salon she was working at and ingratiated himself to her as a lawyer. He began putting thoughts in her head, that Sonny was a no-good bum who didn't treat her the way she deserved to be treated and that she deserved better. Of course, he volunteered to handle her divorce for free. What Sonny didn't know was that Anne had been sleeping with Samjaya for the past six months. But he was going by the name Sam Kent.

Sonny and Anne had two dogs at the time, Anne's female German shepherd and a monster male Great Pyrenees mix that Sonny and the boys adopted recently. Anne didn't want either of them. The boys went to live with Sonny by choice. Anne got a rental with her mom temporarily but then handed her mom off to her brother. Anne got what she wanted—no husband, no kids living with her, no dogs, and a judge to award her thousands in the divorce from a cop. Total freedom which, she said, she totally deserved.

What did Sonny get?

Despair, debt, and emotional pain. He tried not to show it in front of the kids, but occasionally his pain surfaced. Sonny would often awake in the middle of the night crying. He took a vow of celibacy. Just in case Anne took him back, he could tell her that he had not slept with anyone else. She teased him with reconciliation by going out with him dancing or to dinner for about a year. Every time he would have a meet-and-greet date with another woman, Anne would surface and give him hope. Samjaya disappeared from Anne's life just after the divorce. It was like Stockholm syndrome for Sonny. Anne didn't give a shit about him, but he still thought they were meant to be together. After about a year of false hope, they met for dinner at a local brewery/restaurant. Sonny asked Anne to either give him a rope or give him hope. Anne was brutal, really incapable of real emotion. Her depth went about teaspoon depth. Anne told Sonny to stop trying and she was seeing someone. She downplayed her new relationship by saying it had only been about three or 4 dates, but it was actually three or four months. She had been juggling Sonny and this other guy.

Sonny had to pick up his bootstraps and practice what he preached. He had to practice positive thinking and mindfulness. If he really believed that negative thoughts cascade into negative realities, then the inverse was also true. Sonny started drawing, reading, and taking better care of himself physically. He started going to dinner at Luigi's, a local Italian bar/restaurant in Pasadena. Sonny became comfortable being there and talking to people he'd meet there. After a year after the divorce and two years since Anne told him she wasn't in love with him anymore, Sonny was joining the real world again. He'd had a few dates, but no real relationship ever developed mostly because he was in limbo with Anne.

On a Saturday night in February, Sonny was at Luigi's eating by himself and reading a book. He was at one of those tall tables you see at bars but back in a corner. Cops like to sit in the back of rooms so they can constantly survey the scene as people walk around. He spotted a beautiful woman at the bar doing the same thing. She was tall with long dark hair. She turned around as if she could sense that Sonny was looking at her. Sonny recognized her immediately. It was Nurse Simone, the woman who was really nice to him after he had been hit by a car and went to the hospital. She smiled at Sonny and recognized him as well. She stood from her stool at the bar and walked over to Sonny. She was absolutely stunning and carried herself with elegance.

She walked right over and extended her right hand to shake Sonny's hand while saying, "Hello, handsome."

Sonny stood and shook her hand. A vision flashed in his mind while shaking her hand, like when the picture of a memory flashed in your mind, although this wasn't something from this lifetime. As he stood looking down at Simone, he saw them standing on a beach by the ocean. She had a tiara in her hair, and it was very formal. She looked up at him and smiled with unconditional love. She was wearing a white gown with a golden rope-type belt around her waist. They were standing by a Roman or Egyptian city, and Sonny was in some kind of Roman military uniform. It was a vision of their wedding day from another lifetime. For a split second, Sonny wasn't at Luigi's. It was their wedding day from centuries ago. He shook his head and returned to the moment. The smell of the restaurant hit him like a slap in the face. The wonderful smell of garlic, pasta sauce, and wine returned. Sonny didn't believe in the past-life principle. He believed in one soul and one goal, but that was weird.

Sonny and Simone talked for hours at Luigi's. They had a lot in common. She didn't have a *Brady Bunch* childhood either. She was smart and sassy, and the time flew by. It was like his soul recognized hers and vice versa. Finally the bar was closing down. It was almost midnight. They walked to the parking lot to say good night. Sonny gave her a hug and then backed away a couple of steps, saying that it was really nice getting to know her. Then something happened.

Sonny heard a voice in his head say, *Kiss her, dummy.*

It was the first time he had ever actually heard Raguel. For Raguel, it was like he was just thinking out loud.

Call it a nudge; but Sonny replied out loud, "Okay, okay."

Sonny took a few steps back to Simone, and the two embraced. It was a kiss attuned like someone with amnesia suddenly getting their memory back. It was like nothing either had ever experienced before. This went on for a few minutes until the two actually said good night.

Before they broke for the night, Simone said, "You know I saw that, right?"

Sonny asked what she was talking about. She told him that, right before he kissed her, he shook his head and said "Okay, okay." Sonny was stunned.

Uh-oh, what now? he thought. *She is going to think I'm crazy.*

Sonny replied, "Sorry. I guess I was thinking out loud."

Simone told Sonny that she thought it was cute and let him off the hook.

Whew, Sonny thought, *that was close.*

They agreed to see each other again and said good night.

What Sonny didn't know was, when they shook hands, Simone saw the vision that Sonny saw. The supernatural wasn't a crazy concept to Simone. She was an empath. Going back centuries, the women in her lineage were powerful empaths. She didn't share the vision exactly, but she saw it through Sonny's eyes. She let him off the hook when she saw him acknowledge Raguel aloud and then watched Sonny try to explain the behavior. She didn't know everything there was to know about Sonny just by the handshake or the kiss. It wasn't exactly like she downloaded a Sonny file, but she knew something was different about him. Simone could sense the presence of angels around Sonny.

Within a couple of weeks, the two were inseparable. They were with each other whenever time permitted. Luke and Joshua saw their mom sometimes on weekends when she wasn't traveling with her new love interest, Fred. Sonny was at Simone's on those occasions. Sonny even didn't trust his feelings with Anne enough to tell her that he was on antianxiety medication at one time, but he found himself confiding in Simone more and more. Sonny hadn't told her all of the details, but she knew that he had dreams and got nudges. A couple of months went by, and Simone surprised Sonny with a weekend trip up the coast to Monterey. Sonny really needed a getaway. They stayed at a bed-and-breakfast on the ocean.

After spending some time at Point Lobos National Park by the ocean, they returned to the bed-and-breakfast for the night. There was a tall bed in the room with an old boat for a base. There was a stool next to the bed that was there to climb onto the bed. Shortly after climbing into bed, the two were talking and relaxing. They were startled by the sound of the stool sliding across the floor. Simone knew that Sonny usually had ghosts around, but now this was real. She held on tight and asked Sonny if he heard that.

Of course he did, but Sonny told her, "You get used to it."

They ignored the sound, and Simone was mildly concerned. The ghost, however, wanted to be acknowledged. There was a nightstand right next to the bed. Four distinct knocks sounded on the wooden nightstand. Can't ignore that. Sonny had heard knocks countless times but never four. He had hoped it was the archangel Uriel because Uriel was known as the fourth angel, but it wasn't.

Sonny saw a spirit in the front doorway. Her body was transparent, half in the room and half outside. She had short dark hair and a translucent blouse. She was medium height, about five feet, six inches, and thin. Simone asked Sonny if he saw anything.

He said, "Yes, there is the spirit of a woman in the doorway."

Simone asked Sonny what her name was. Before Sonny could even think, the name Tracy popped in his head. This wasn't the first time Sonny had ever seen a ghost. He saw an apparition in Minnesota once on a family trip to see Anne's uncles. That ghost was just a remnant though, a memory. Tracy was interactive. Tracy was different.

The heater had stopped working, and the room drew colder. Tracy's mouth wasn't moving, but Sonny could hear her, much like when Sonny was a kid and he saw his grandfather in a dream. Tracy told Sonny to open the door. Sonny refused. Simone asked Sonny if Tracy was saying anything, and he told her that Tracy wanted him to open the door. Simone held on tighter and told Sonny not to do it. Who knew what she wanted to let in? Sonny told Tracy he wasn't going to open the door and she had to leave. Tracy replied that she was the one who lived there and they needed to go. Tracy then disappeared, and the heater kicked back on in the room. The next day, Simone and Sonny did some touristy shit and hiked through some redwoods in the area, lunch, and sightseeing. They had one more night in the haunted hotel room. When they got back, there was no sign of Tracy the angry ghost. They felt comfortable doing what adults do.

Sonny was sitting up in the bed, and Simone was cuddled around him, almost asleep. Sonny closed his eyes, and suddenly he was in Egypt. He was in a room with no doors but with pillars of salt and stone. It was a big open room that overlooked the ocean from an elevated structure/home. It wasn't a shack or a shanty but a mansion. He was sitting on a large bed with his back resting against a wall and his arms stretched out across pillows. His lower body was under blankets. There were two young boys running around the room playing. Simone was standing by the edge of the room wearing a nightgown and looking out at the landscape of the beach and the ocean. It was a sunny morning, and Sonny was at peace. Sonny opened his eyes, and he was back in the present, in bed with Simone at the bed-and-breakfast. It was a similar experience as when he shook Simone's hand for the first time.

Simone shifted in bed and said, "I think we were married in a former life."

This shocked Sonny. The timing of that statement could not be coincidental. He just had that vision, and she said that? Sonny sat up more erect in the bed and asked her to reiterate what she just said.

Simone replied, "I saw it too, the beach, the ocean, the kids…all of it."

Sonny was in shock. He said aloud, "I don't fucking believe this."

Simone knew things about Sonny that she could not possibly know. For example, Simone told Sonny that he had the essence of an angel. She also told him that he and his boys had "soul contracts" that were ancient. When Sonny was away from Luke or Joshua, their balance was disrupted. Sonny thought that was true because, when the boys weren't with him, at their mom's, he did feel a weird shift in energy. This wasn't some psychic con or bad TV show; this was real. Sonny's spiritual neurons and synapses were firing when he was around Simone.

Sonny and Simone talked a lot on the drive back home to Burbank. Sonny could finally talk to someone about his spiritual experiences in life without thinking he was crazy. For Simone, it was welcomed too. She could do the same. Simone was also a descendant of light. She was a healer, an empath, and an energy worker. Simone was of the lineage to Saint Elizabeth, the mother of John the Baptist and cousin to Mary of Nazareth. Luke 1:13 tells the story of the archangel Gabriel appearing to Saint Elizabeth's husband, Zacharias, to tell him that he and his wife would conceive a child and that his name was to be John. Zacharias doubted Archangel Gabriel because he and his wife were way past the child-conceiving age. As a punishment, Zacharias lost the ability to speak for about five months until the child was born. Elizabeth was patient and kind, slow to anger, loving, and beautiful. She was everything that people say in their wedding vows. Plus, she was smart. It was believed that Saint Elizabeth was buried in a monastery in Jerusalem.

The descendants of Saint Elizabeth carried the same character traits. They had a bright light and, as such, didn't have an easy life, like Simone. Both of her parents spent time in prison. She was passed around from family member to family member during childhood. She learned survival and coping skills from an early age. All descendants of light experience abandonment issues because watchers work hard to separate them from all loved ones and support systems at an early age. If a DOL survives, he or she is the strongest of the strong. They are uncommon even among special people. Neither Sonny nor Simone knew anything about Simone's lineage, but Sonny instinctively recognized the connection. He remembered what the angel Johel had told him when he first explained what a DOL was, that some had a more profound connection with their gifts and some chalked it up to intuition or gut feelings. Simone had a difficult life but wasn't quite on the watchers' radar like Sonny was. She hadn't fought demons in Canada or been transported by an angel, but that was about to change. Sonny did confide in her on the trip to Monterey. There were some epiphanies, but he didn't spill all of the beans.

Sonny went back to work when they returned home. He had Luke and Josh most of the time, except for an occasional weekend with their mom. They were ten and twelve years old and getting bigger. They did not appear to have his curse of stunted growth like he did. Sonny wanted the boys to have a more normal childhood than his. He knew that someday they might be asked to be soldiers for God as he had, but he wanted to prolong that for as long as possible. They were beyond athletic and smart and played sports like all of the other kids. The lineage of Moses is a high-profile line for angels and watchers alike. Sonny's father dropped the ball in preparing Sonny for the battles. Sonny's father sedated himself with tranquilizers to the point that he fell off the radar. Sonny was determined that he would be better. Anne was happy with her new life—no ghosts and no dreams that she was possessed. She not only left Sonny; she left the spiritual cardio that she had to do while she was a part of Sonny's life. Sonny knew that was hard for Anne.

How many wives have to put up with ghosts knocking in the house or demonic pursuits of her husband and everyone that her husband loves? Sonny contemplated getting involved with Simone. Would she be okay with this challenge that came with being with Sonny? They didn't have to wait long to find out.

About a month later, Sonny had worked a Friday-night patrol swing shift. He got home late and went to bed immediately. He didn't sleep well usually, but on this occasion, he crashed quickly. In his dream, Simone was on her bed in about the middle. Sonny was standing near the bed. Simone reached for him with one hand while clutching the end of the bed with the other. She was trying to pull away from something but wasn't able to.

She screamed, "Sonny!" as something was dragging her deep into the middle of the bed as if there was a hole to hell in the bed, but she had a firm grip on the bed.

Sonny replied, "Elizabeth!" as he grabbed her arms and body and began pulling her off the bed.

Sonny sensed that there was a presence of a demon pulling against him, and he awoke. It wasn't a long dream, but it was terrifying and sent the message that now Simone wasn't safe. It was about 1:00 a.m., but he called Simone anyway. She answered the phone and told Sonny that she wasn't in bed but had fallen asleep on the couch. She was shaken a bit by the late call and the dream. Sonny told her that he was going to send her the archangel Michael, and everything was going to be okay for her to go back to sleep.

Sonny got off the phone and spoke aloud as if Michael was in the room with him, not like a fictional character or a stranger. Sonny told Archangel Michael that he needed him to go to Simone and protect her. Sonny spoke plainly as if he was speaking to a brother. The next morning, Simone met Sonny for breakfast, and he felt obligated to reveal what he knew about the existence of angels and what he had been tasked to do by the angel Johel.

Sonny spoke about the dream and what he thought it meant. Simone told Sonny that, after she spoke to Sonny last night, she went to bed. She said that, when she first awoke to Sonny's phone call last night, she was a little rattled. Then hearing about his dream, she was a little scared, but then a peace fell over her like there was an angel there protecting her. Sonny told her that he did call aloud for the archangel Michael to look out for her. Sonny asked her if her middle name was Elizabeth by any chance.

She said, "No. Why?"

Sonny told her, in his dream, it was her but he called her Elizabeth. Neither knew what that meant but were curious. Sonny told Simone about his experiences with the angel Johel and his duties as a descendant of light. Simone felt that everyone was responsible to use the gifts that God had given them. It took a few minutes to explain the whole situation, and Simone sat in silence for a few moments after. Being open to the supernatural is one thing, but accepting that someone is a soldier for the Holy Spirit and has to fight demons is something else entirely.

It's a lot to take on, but Simone told Sonny, "So we just have to keep you alive for the next three years...No problem."

Sonny asked if she was sure. She was going to be on the watchers' radar, and he didn't want her to possibly become collateral damage. Simone loved Sonny. She recognized the soul connection. Her third eye was opening more the more time she spent with Sonny as well. Simone had always felt a pull to Egypt as much as Sonny felt a pull to Rome. Their history together went back far beyond this lifetime.

Simone wasn't in nursing anymore. She owned a small independent health clinic that provided different wellness services. She saw all manner of clients/patients. She did everything from giving a B12 shot to energy work. Simone was successful and self-made. The next Monday, after breakfast with Sonny and learning the truth about the watchers and DOLs, a strange client came into the clinic. A woman claimed that she was an independent exorcist of demonic possessions. This woman told Simone that she had been working with a family toward exorcising their fifteen-year-old daughter. Simone asked this woman what brought her to Simone's clinic. The woman asked to use Simone's clinic after hours to perform the final exorcism ceremony. Kind of a coincidence considering Sonny's dream just a couple of days ago. Simone told the woman not only no but fuck no. The demon was attached to this woman and walked into the clinic with her. Simone told the woman to get out and take the demon that was attached to her when she went. Like Sonny told her, the watchers harassed anyone he cared about. As soon as the woman left, Simone called Sonny.

Simone told Sonny what had just happened.

Without hesitation, Sonny said the name Galadriel. "It was real, and the demon's name is Galadriel."

Simone asked him how he knew that. He told her that name just popped into his head. She asked if he had ever heard that name before.

Sonny said no. "No clue, but probably a nudge from Raguel."

They were both at work and agreed to talk more about it later. When she had a free moment, she looked the name up on the Internet. She discovered that there was such a fallen angel named Galadriel. Not only that, but he was one of Lucifer's top lieutenants and the worst of the worst. Simone was understandably shaken. Also, how did Sonny pull that name out of thin air? All this shit was becoming too real for Simone. At the end of the business day, she burned sage and incense and did some other things to cleanse the clinic of possible negative energy.

Sonny met Simone at her shop after her business closed. Sonny did tell Simone about Johel and Raguel just a couple of days ago, but if she was going to stay with him, Sonny felt like she should know the whole truth. Sonny asked her to go with him, and they took her car. They usually took Simone's car because she had a beautiful white Range Rover, and Sonny had an alimony-induced old Subaru. Simone asked where they were going, and he asked that she trusted him. He took her to Holy Cross Church, where he had met with the angel Johel a couple of times. They pulled into the empty parking lot and got out of the car. Simone asked what they were doing there.

Sonny replied, "We're here to get some answers."

They walked up to the door of the church, and the door was locked, not ajar like it used to be when he saw Johel. Sonny shook the door and looked around the facade of the building like he was looking for an entrance, but it appeared secure. Sonny called aloud for Johel, but there was no answer.

Simone told Sonny, "I guess he's not here."

They got back in her car, Sonny in the driver's seat and she in the passenger's. He started the car and started to put the car in drive as Simone was asking him what they were going to do now. A bright light burst into the back seat, and Simone stopped talking. Sonny looked over at Simone, and she was catatonic like a mannequin. Sonny turned around and saw Johel in the back seat.

Johel told Sonny, "I'm not sure if you know how this works, but you don't summon angels at your will like some parlor trick to impress a girl."

Sonny told Johel that he put a target on the back of every person he got close to, and now he had put a spotlight on Simone. Johel explained that apparently Simone knew the risks and chose to be with him anyway, and wasn't that enough? Sonny told Johel that Simone was different from any other woman that he had ever met, and he thought she may have been a descendant of light. Johel told Sonny that he was aware that Simone was different. That was because she was of the lineage of Elizabeth and Zechariah, but that didn't give Sonny the right to choose whom Johel decided to reveal himself to. Sonny told Johel that he needed help and that the demon Galadriel made his presence known in Simone's shop and that could not be a coincidence. Johel told Sonny that watchers were aware of all descendants of light and protecting them was his responsibility. Until a demon made a threat to a DOL's life, humans had the free will to resist them. Johel told Sonny that when that happened, he'd be in touch. Johel disappeared in a burst of light, and Simone awoke, continuing what she was saying before Johel appeared. Being in the presence of an angel was fatiguing, even still for Sonny. Sonny was slumped in the driver's seat and kind of nodding off like he was about to fall asleep. Simone asked him if he was okay.

Sonny replied, "Looks like we're on our own for now."

Sonny had a choice to make. He wanted to be honest with Simone, but knowing that she was a descendant of light and what that came with was a huge download. Did he tell her? Sonny was Catholic, but he wasn't sure who Elizabeth and Zachariah were either. Would she even believe him? He had just under three years left until his forty-third birthday. The endgame was coming, and he could use the help.

As they drove back to her shop where his car was parked, these thoughts swirled in his head. It was a very quiet ride. They pulled into the lot and parked. Simone started to get out of the car, and Sonny told her to wait a minute. She closed the door and asked what was wrong. Sonny told her that she needed to hear something. She looked nervous.

Sonny said, "Here goes nothing."

He told her that he had just spoken to Johel and he wasn't happy that Sonny tried to make him reveal himself to Simone, but he did provide some cryptic information. Sonny told her that she was of the line of Elizabeth and Zechariah, whoever that was, and she was a DOL. Simone told Sonny that Elizabeth was the mother of John the Baptist, so it made sense that Elizabeth was touched by God. Sonny told her that it was pretty clear that he worked at the behest of the angels, not the other way around. Simone asked how the interaction between Sonny and Raguel worked. He explained that he didn't communicate with Raguel, but Raguel was keeping him alive. Raguel could give him nudges and hunches, but that was how he received information from him.

Sonny chuckled and told her, "Don't worry. Raguel closes his celestial eyes when we are intimate. He's not interested in that activity."

Simone turned toward the back seat of her car and said, "You mean there was an angel in my ba…ck seat?"

Her last couple of words were drawn out as she noticed a strange object in the back seat that was not left there before. She directed Sonny's attention to it and asked him what it was. It was cylindrical and about twelve inches long. It was wooden but had gold Arabic-type symbols the length of it.

Both exited the car, and Sonny opened the back door and looked down at the object for a couple of seconds, wondering what the hell it was. Simone told him that it looked like Johel left him a present.

Sonny replied, "More like a responsibility." Sonny said, "Fuck it," and reached into the back seat and picked it up. As he inspected it in his hand, he said, "Am I supposed to say some magic words or some shit? Will it glow when demons are around? Will it only appear when needed or if I'm worthy?"

All those clichés were questions in his mind and what they could be used for. Simone was good at filling in the blanks for Sonny. Whether it was interpreting a dream or recognizing a nudge, she was able to translate celestial messages for him. Sonny handed the object to her, but as she reached to accept it, a little jolt of electricity reached out to her hand and shocked her. She stepped back, stunned a little, but was okay. She told Sonny apparently he was the only one meant to hold it, but she did feel a message.

Sonny asked, "What's that?"

She replied, "Try thinking, 'Reveal yourself.'"

Sonny acknowledged what Simone said with a head nod and said, "Here goes."

He closed his eyes and thought the phrase. As he did that, the twelve-inch cylindrical dowel transformed into a six-foot staff. It was glowing gold and felt warm to the touch. The Arabic letters were an electric purple color. Basically the coolest thing either of them had ever seen.

Sonny said, "I guess it's a good thing I've practiced with a staff in martial arts since I was twelve years old."

Simone told Sonny that she was pretty sure that was the staff of Moses and asked what Sonny thought it meant.

Sonny replied, "I think it means shit is going to get really dangerous," and asked her if she wanted out.

Simone said, "No way." She was in it no matter what.

Sonny was relieved to hear that and told her that he loved her. Then he asked, "How do I close this thing?"

The two went into her shop and stared at the staff for a little while as Sonny tried to think of phrases to get it to retract back into the more compact twelve-inch version. Simone suggested that maybe the staff didn't respond to phrases and that it was as simple as it responded to Sonny's will. Sonny asked what she meant. Simone told Sonny to just tell it to close. Sonny looked at the staff and focused on what he wanted the staff to do. In an instant, the staff retracted back to its original form.

Sonny said aloud, "An owner's manual would be nice."

Sonny and Simone agreed that they would stay close and report anything strange to each other. Sonny had Lucas and Joshua at his house most of the time, and Simone had two kids of her own at her place. So living together until this was over wasn't practical, but they agreed to stay in constant contact.

Simone went home and tried to process what she had experienced. It was a lot to take in, not just about her relationship with Sonny, but the truth about her own lineage as well. Sonny had been prepared for the supernatural his whole life, so it was different for him. Simone was empathic and a DOL, but she wasn't harassed by watchers. Now she was on their radar. It didn't take long for her to be reminded that she was a person of interest. Simone went to bed that night nestled with her standard poodle as usual. Her room wasn't cluttered with decorative things, but she did have this large decorative letter *S* in the room that looked like something that used to be on the roof of an old motel in the 1970s. It was pink with LED lights that weren't even plugged in. It was leaned against the wall but kind of tilted and pretty steadily standing up.

At 2:43 a.m., Simone awoke to the sound of the letter *S* hitting the ground. It made a thunderous sound that would awake the neighborhood. She also had a tablet on a nightstand next to her bed that was off when she went to bed. The tablet was on and playing a movie with the volume turned way up. Her dog, Harry, was at the edge of the bed, barking. Simone sat up in bed, and the unsettling feeling of not being alone in the room fell upon her like heavy rain in Seattle. About five seconds later, the tablet turned off. The dog stopped barking, and the room fell silent. Simone got out of bed and slowly walked over to the letter *S* decoration and stood it up. She didn't call Sonny that night though. It was over, and she didn't want to tell him how scared she was. She had just told him she was going to stay at her shop when they found the staff, so she'd wait till the morning. She settled back into bed and tried to get some sleep.

The next morning, she spoke to Sonny about what happened last night. She was a little shaken but okay for the most part. Every call for service Sonny went on, he had to wonder: Would this be the average garden-variety threat that came with being a cop, or could it be a supernatural threat? Simone also had to be more aware and alert. Everyone that came into the clinic had to be a little more scrutinized. Were they coming in for help, or were they bringing in a watcher attached to them? She wasn't incarnate with an angel and didn't have the staff of Moses either. Call after call, Sonny faced more and more threatening situations in patrol. He was working as a patrol sergeant and wasn't usually the first officer on the scene of calls, but lately dangerous calls had been finding him.

Just driving along in Burbank, stopped at a red light in his police car, Sonny saw a man walk out of a liquor store; and his attention was drawn to the pistol in his right hand with his arm extended down at his leg. Sonny threw the car in park and jumped out. Sonny drew his duty weapon and ordered the man to drop the gun. The man looked at Sonny but with a thousand-yard stare. Sonny could see that the man's head was tilting back and forth like someone was whispering in his ear.

Louder and louder, Sonny shouted his verbal commands, "Drop the gun!"

The man shook his head like shaking off a mosquito or trapped in a dream. He became conscious of the situation and suddenly complied with Sonny's orders. He dropped to his knees, and Sonny took him into custody without resistance.

A couple of shifts later, Sonny was driving past a local hospital, and his attention was drawn to what ended up being a chair thrown through a fourth-story window. Sonny again threw the police car in park and ran into the hospital. There were staff and people running on the fourth floor. One of the nurses directed Sonny to a room where a patient had taken a nurse hostage and broken out the window. Sonny peaked his head around the doorway to the room and saw a man facing the door standing by the back window in the room. He was a bald older White guy wearing a hospital gown. There was a nurse standing in front of him. He had his left arm around her chest area, pulling her toward him. He had a broken piece of glass in his right hand, and it was pressed against the front of her throat. The man was about five feet, eleven inches, and the nurse was about five feet, six inches. Sonny thought he had enough line of sight of the man's head for a headshot, but that wasn't the problem. The two were standing up against the broken window. If Sonny took a headshot, they might both go out the window. The man was frantic and irate.

He was yelling, "I'll cut this bitch's throat!"

Sonny spoke calmly and rationally to the man in an attempt to deescalate the situation, but it wasn't working. It was, however, giving Sonny time and other police officers to arrive.

There was an adjoining doorway to the room on the man's right and Sonny's left as Sonny saw the situation. Sonny had a couple of SWAT guys on his patrol team that were very squared away. Officer Dave Nettle had taken a small three-man team to that other doorway. Officer Nettle was a SWAT guy and a veteran officer. Sonny trusted him. He was older, midforties, but one of those guys that lived CrossFit and was damn good with a pistol. With Nettle to his left and the suspect in front of him, they had the guy triangulated. Yeah, Nettle could take a shot with his pistol, but the bad guy could still pull her out the window with him if he wanted. Nettle deducted that he had to lock up this guy's system so that Sonny could pull her to safety.

Because the bad guy was focused on Sonny, he didn't even see Officer Nettle's team to his right. Officer Nettle took a kneeling position with his Taser. A big tall officer,

Alan Worthington, stood tall above him with his handgun drawn in case the Taser didn't work. Worthington wasn't on SWAT, but at that range, it didn't matter. Sonny liked Worthington too. He was a happy-go-lucky guy whose personality didn't match his size. He was about six feet, seven inches, and 275 pounds but didn't have a mean bone in his body. Nettle's plan went together fairly quickly.

He told Worthington, "I'll go low, and you go high, and I'll hit him with the Taser."

Boom, Nettle shot his Taser, and the prongs hit the guy in his right thigh and his upper torso. The bad guy's body was locked up, and he was frozen like Alaskan ice. He even extended his right arm a little. That gave separation from the nurse's throat with the piece of broken glass. Sonny moved to her and pulled her away from him. Nettle's team took the guy into custody without any more resistance.

Sonny was having lunch at a restaurant in downtown Burbank with his friend Sergeant Brentavious. Dispatch radioed Sonny that a cab driver was driving to the big hotel across the street from where Sonny was with a fair. Apparently the cab driver's mic was open, and what was happening inside the cab was being fed to police dispatch via the cab dispatcher. There was a male in the back seat of the cab. He told the cab driver that he had several guns on him and he was going to enter the hotel and kill as many people as he could before killing himself. It was a really smart move by the cab driver to key his mic open. Sonny and Brentavious ran from the restaurant and took positions behind parked cars on the street, waiting for the cab to arrive. The driver's position and ETA being provided by the police dispatcher gave them almost a countdown to the suspect's arrival. Minutes later, the cab arrived. The suspect exited the back seat of the cab and looked at the hotel that he was about to shoot up.

Sergeant Brentavious shouted, "Police! Don't move!"

The suspect was completely surprised. He turned around to see two police officers with their guns drawn at him as the cab he just arrived in sped away. There he was standing in the street contemplating his fate. Sonny and Brentavious could see the gun in his waistband, and his hands were down to his sides.

Brentavious shouted, "Go down to your knees!"

But the man just had a thousand-yard stare, like he was deliberately indifferent to their presence. He didn't even see a police officer running at him from his left side. The officer tackled him, and two or three guns were ejected from the suspect's possession. After wrestling with him for a couple of seconds, he was handcuffed without a shot being fired. It was a bonehead move for the other officer to tackle a guy in the middle of a shoot-out like the OK Corral, but it worked out. Demons were whispering in people's ears more and more, and these calls were happening all the time. How long could Sonny keep this up, and what harassment was Simone going to have to endure? Could he make it to his forty-third birthday?

Sonny had those questions in his mind and handled his calls like he was a regular cop, but he always had the staff of Moses on him in case any call went celestial. He practiced with the staff when he was by himself and tried to get proficient at it even though it didn't come with an owner's manual. This went on for almost a year. Dangerous call after dangerous call, watchers were trying to kill him at every turn. Sonny never called in sick and hardly took a day off. His pride wouldn't let him hide. There were many initiators in the journey to Revelations in the Bible. The death or corruption of the seventieth son of the seventieth son was but one of those triggers. But it was the most important one from Sonny's perspective. The watchers had tried to kill him several times, successfully once. They had tried to neuter his mind with panic and anxiety. They harassed and menaced his ex-wife. They had gone after his children. They had made their presence known and threatened his girlfriend, Simone. Of course, he chose the profession of police officer and provided the watchers opportunities to fulfill the prophecy. Sonny had warrior DNA. Now, as he was nearing the end of the prophecy, they were in a full-court press to kill him. It had been almost a year since he was given the staff by Johel, and he had battled life-threatening situations nonstop. The good news was Sonny's family and friends stopped being a focus for the watchers.

Simone had a successful clinic. She was very good at her job, and her revenue did not go unnoticed. She often would get visits from headhunters from large corporations with offers to buy her business so that it could be absorbed into theirs. One busy Saturday afternoon, a woman walked in the business whom Simone had not seen before. She got new clients and walk-ins, but most of the clientele were repeat customers. This woman was about six feet tall and had long blond hair. She was about thirty-five years old and looked like she could talk her way out of any traffic ticket. She was wearing a light-pink business suit/skirt and spoke with a European accent.

She came in and didn't ask to speak to the owner like the usual corporate headhunter. She approached Simone and introduced herself like she knew it was Simone's business. The woman introduced herself as Sari and said that she represented a large medical firm and was interested in buying the clinic. In the past, offers from other companies were decent but nothing that Simone couldn't refuse. They sat down in Simone's office, and Sari came right to the point. She slid a piece of paper across the desk and asked Simone to open it. Simone did and looked at the number. It was $3.7 million. There was a brief moment of silence as Simone tried to process the figure she was looking at.

Sari looked around Simone's office and said, "I can see you are infatuated with Egypt. Take the money and take the trip."

There were numerous pictures and small figurines of Egypt in Simone's office. Sari told Simone she would have the papers drawn up for Simone's lawyers, but there wouldn't be any funny business in the contract. Within a week, Sari was back with the paperwork and the check. The check payable to Simone was by ARK Health Clinics. Sari and Simone shook hands, and the deal was done. She sold the business that she started about eight years ago, but she was finally able to travel to Egypt as she had always wanted. She handed the keys to Sari, got in her Range Rover, and drove away. Sari locked the door and was in there by herself.

Sari said aloud, "You can come out now," as beautiful large pink wings emerged from her back.

Sari was the angel Sariel, and with a burst of golden light, the angel Johel appeared.

Johel told Sariel, "Thank you for doing that. It will be better for Sonny if she's not here for this."

Sariel replied, "Happy to be of service."

The two disappeared with their wings engulfing themselves into spheres of light that matched their wings.

Sonny was very proud of Simone for the sale of the business and happy that she planned a trip to Egypt. She was going with a large group of people from the US. There were tour packages that included a houseboat, almost like a cruise ship that travels along the Nile with touristy stops along the way. It was about six months to a year away, which might coincide with his forty-third birthday. It was about a three-week adventure. Sonny loved Simone and wanted to go with her, but the fact that she might not be around for the possible final showdown brought him some comfort. If he survived, there would be time for them after. Sonny had no delusions of grandeur. He knew that there was the possibility that he might not come out on top. Yes, he had been given the staff, but it had been over a year since he last spoke to Johel. He'd been dodging bullets ever since. Raguel was working overtime giving him precognitive nudges for his safety. His coworkers started calling him the "shit magnet." He also wasn't sure how to use the damn staff.

Sonny was working an overtime shift on a Friday night in an area known for house parties and underage drinking. Sonny and a couple of other officers responded to a fight in Glendale. When they arrived, there were people running from the house and speeding off in cars. This was typical when One Time arrived at house parties. They called the police One Time because they were notorious for telling people, "If we have to come back here one more time…" The fight was over, but officers checked IDs and the state of minors. After about fifteen to thirty minutes, Sonny found himself standing in the living room babysitting a couple of the adults whom they were checking for warrants on. Other officers were walking in and out of the house performing various tasks. Everything seemed like it was coming to a close on this particular call. For a brief moment, Sonny found himself alone in the house. There were three or four people in the living room. Three people were sitting on the couch, and there may have been one or two others in different chairs or seated on the floor. Sonny was deeper into the room than the people he was babysitting, almost to the kitchen. That is to say they were closer to the front door.

A man known as David, who hadn't spoken a word the entire time the police were there, stood up from the couch and walked over to the front door. He closed the door and locked the dead bolt, trapping Sonny inside with them. David was a scary dude. He was a Black guy about five feet, ten inches tall, about 240 pounds, and a prison buff. He wasn't dressed like the other people at the party. He was wearing a plaid flannel shirt, Wrangler jeans, and Roper boots. This guy did not fit in with the others. The others in the room that were with him were even scared of him.

He turned around after closing the door and said, "Let's have a word, Lucas."

Sonny hadn't gone by that name since he was about twelve years old. Officers were pounding on the door trying to gain entry, realizing that Sonny was trapped in the residence.

Sonny told David, "How do you know that name?"

David replied, "Well, I've killed you once. I know everything about you."

Sonny replied, "Azazel."

Azazel said, "Bingo, dummy."

Sonny reached inside his bulletproof vest where he kept the staff of Moses.

Azazel said, "Don't bother, kid. I wasn't going to kill you right now."

Sonny asked Azazel what he wanted. Azazel told Sonny that he wanted the end of mankind of course. Azazel told Sonny that he was not going to make it to his forty-third birthday.

Sonny responded by saying, "I'm not going to play your games or jump through your hoops."

Azazel told Sonny that he would if he liked it or not. Azazel said, "Rats can't resist cheese."

Sonny said, "What the fuck does that mean?"

Azazel told Sonny that his course was set and he would die horribly. Sonny told Azazel that he could open that door and twenty cops would be in his ass.

Azazel replied, "You'd have twenty dead cops. Please do."

As Azazel spoke, Sonny noticed that there were two voices reverberating. This wasn't Azazel's form; he was clearly possessing this person David. Sonny didn't want to get in a big fight with this guy or any of the other people in the room, and he didn't want to get any cops hurt. The front door to the residence was kicked open by a big police officer, and cops started to come in thinking that Sonny was in a knockdown, drag-out fight. Sonny was squared off in a fighting stance with David. David, the man Azazel was possessing, shook his head and was disoriented. He put his arms up and asked where he was. He was handcuffed immediately but insisted he didn't know how he got there. Sonny could tell that Azazel was gone. Sonny told the other officers that they had a misunderstanding and to release him. David looked intimidating, but he was actually an electrician that lived in Pasadena. Azazel had taken his body earlier that day, and his wife had left twenty messages on his cell phone wondering where he was.

Sonny and the other officers left the call shortly and continued their shift. Sonny was a little confused. He was asking himself questions about Azazel's intentions. Was he just trying to scare Sonny? Was Sonny putting other officers in danger just by being a police officer> Did this mean that Sonny's family was in greater danger? Why, why, why? Sonny was forty-two years old and had been on LAPD for twenty-one years. Back then, cops could retire at twenty-five years of service without any age penalties and could collect their retirement. Without telling any of his coworkers, he went to see a retirement counselor for the state pension system. Sonny found out that he could almost buy the remaining time he had to get to the twenty-five benchmark by using his sick time. (Sonny hardly ever called in sick in twenty-one years.) He would just have to do about six more months. He could retire about a week from his forty-third birthday.

Sonny thought to himself, *Great. I can enjoy my retirement for about a week before I'm killed by demons.*

Sonny told Simone and his mom, but that was about it.

Sonny had started developing a relationship with his sisters and brother again after the divorce from Anne, but they didn't hang out a lot. He was very close with his mother, Helen. His father was still shacked up in Reno with a woman Sonny didn't know or care about. Sonny had Luke and Joshua a week on and a week off with his ex-wife. The boys were starting to see and talk to their mother more. Sonny told the boys that, being fourteen and twelve, they were responsible for their own relationship with their mother. Sonny told them that Anne left him, not them, and encouraged them to be with their mom. So far, the boys weren't tormented by the watchers and were basically normal kids, except the occasional pushy ghost that wanted to be noticed in the house.

As far as Sonny was concerned, he learned something from his conversation with Azazel at the house party. It meant that they were focused on him and not Simone or the boys. Sonny planned to retire in six months just before his forty-third birthday to keep anyone else from getting hurt as collateral damage. Even if it was a week before, if it prevented anyone else from getting hurt, it was worth it for Sonny. The next six months weren't going to be a cakewalk. Simone was really the only person he confided in. She was an empath, and she shined. Father Tim was only trying to help years ago when he told Sonny not to shine. If he did that, he would attract attention. Simone was different. She knew that Sonny had to accept and embrace that he was different and it was okay. For Sonny, it was like she gave him permission to be who he was without judgment. But Sonny was a spiritual radiation area that was hazardous to anyone that was in his area of influence. Simone knew the risks and loved him anyway.

Call after call and shift after shift, the devil chased Sonny to the exit door of his police career. A couple of weeks away from his birthday, July 2012, he was almost there. Simone left for her trip to Egypt. The boys were at their mom's. Sonny was ready for the endgame. Azazel stepped into a married man one afternoon in Inglewood, California, a computer programmer with a seemingly normal life and a normal wife. The man and his wife got into a verbal argument when he got home after work, which led to her calling 911 (kind of to be expected when a man is possessed by a demon). The husband allowed it because this was just an elaborate plan by Azazel to get Sonny to respond.

As luck would have it, a patrol car was in the area and marked the arrival on the scene almost immediately. The husband refused to allow the police to enter the residence and took his wife hostage at knifepoint. The stand-off ensued, with the officers requesting a supervisor and a hostage negotiator. Sonny was a sergeant and responded. The hostage negotiator got the man on the phone, and he refused to speak to the officer. The suspect demanded to speak to a supervisor in person. Sonny and another officer with an AR15 long rifle approached the house through the open garage roll-up door. The interior man door to the inside of the house was propped open. When they peeked inside the house, they saw a man standing behind a woman, holding a large kitchen knife to her neck. Sonny called to the man to let her go.

The man's eyes lit up red; and he replied, "Hello, Lucas."

Sonny said, "Just let her go, and we'll talk."

Azazel replied, "All these people are collateral damage unless you sacrifice yourself."

As Azazel spoke, Sonny could smell the strong odor of gasoline inside the house. Sonny told Azazel to let the woman go, and he would take her place.

Azazel replied, "Not now, but you'll have your chance soon."

The man had a lighter in his left hand and flicked the flame on. He then tossed it on the ground that was covered in standing gasoline. It ignited quickly, and the house started to go up in flames. The suspect's eyes returned to a blue color as Azazel's spirit left his body and the suspect's consciousness returned. He was confused and disoriented, but that didn't last long. The officer that was with Sonny put a round through the suspect's forehead. He dropped the knife and dropped to the floor. They grabbed the woman and pulled her out of the house as it started burning to the ground. The other officer, Darren, asked Sonny after why the suspect called him Lucas and what the hell he was talking about with all the sacrifice and shit. Sonny dismissed it by saying how he would know what was in the mind of a crazy man.

Sonny got back into his police cruiser after the call to decompress, but he was not alone. The angel Johel was sitting in the back seat.

He scared the shit out of Sonny when he said aloud, "Hello, Sonny."

Sonny turned around and replied, "Jesus, you scared the shit out of me."

Johel said, "I'm not Jesus, but we are on the same team."

Sonny asked why he hasn't shown himself in the last year since giving him the Moses staff. Sonny told Johel that he had been getting chased by the devil on every call for the last year. Johel told Sonny that he wasn't the only descendant of light that was putting in work for God.

Sonny told Johel that he had a couple of hundred questions for him, starting with, "How do I use the staff?"

Johel replied, "Think of it like a magic wand that you can use as a blunt object."

Sonny asked Johel if there was something else about the forty-third prophecy thing that he didn't know about, like a sacrifice component. Johel told him that, besides being killed or corrupted before his forty-third birthday to kick-start Revelations, if Sonny sacrificed his life, the prophecy would be satisfied.

"It would fulfill the prophecy without jumpstarting the Apocalypse?" Sonny asked.

Johel told Sonny to kind of think of it like a push. "Neither heaven nor hell wins. Everything just keeps spinning the way it is." Johel told Sonny that Lucifer must have been scared.

Sonny asked, "Why is that?"

Johel told Sonny that Azazel would not have made that offer if they thought they would be successful at killing Sonny before his birthday.

Sonny said, "Oh, well, that's great. The only one that loses is himself." Sonny asked Johel, "What do I do?"

Johel replied, "Don't die."

Johel disappeared into a golden sphere of light, leaving Sonny just as confused as he was before.

Sonny drove back to the station and never sat in another patrol car again. That was the last day of his police career. He burned a couple of days of sick time and never looked back. He didn't even go back for his retirement ceremony. His friend Brentavious stopped by his house to give him his retirement badge and certificate. Sonny had a week to go and was all alone by choice. He didn't want anyone to get hurt in the wake of what was surely to come. Besides walking the dog, he hardly left the house. The only problem was that he was stuck in an anxiety feedback loop, obsessing about the catastrophe that he thought was imminent. Isolated physically by choice and focused on a future unknown that hadn't even happened yet, he was playing right into the devil's hands, round and round in his head, isolated and alone. He asked himself if he'd done the right thing by sending everyone away from him for their own safety.

Then came August 8, 2012, a day before his birthday. If he survived it, the prophecy would be a thing of his past. He awoke to a quiet house but with loud thoughts of the unknown. About 9:00 a.m. in LA and 5:00 p.m. in Egypt, Sonny's phone rang, and it was Simone. Like a bad dream, his mind awoke when he heard her voice, and he was present in reality instead of trapped in a corner of his mind full of fear. She was comforting and encouraging. Just the very contact with her inspired him to get up and fight—fight for his mind, fight for his life, and fight for his family. Sonny got off the phone with Simone and picked up the staff of Moses. He drove up the coast a bit to a forest of huge redwood trees in a national park. He walked out into the trees with enthusiasm. He asked himself that, if the staff responded to his will, maybe that was a metaphor for the trials and struggles he had been through his entire life. His thoughts had always manifested into his reality, for good or for bad. The devil tries to influence people by whispering into their ears and altering and weakening their will. Could it be that simple? Did it all come down to will-power? Fear, joy, anger, and love—all those feelings are pre-cipitated by thinking.

He thought, "Mindfulness, is that it?"

He held up the staff and willed it to extend. In an instant and a brilliant display of light, the staff opened to be six feet long. Again it had a golden glow with pale-blue Arabic letters. He commanded the sky to thunder, and it did. He commanded it to lightning, and a bolt came down and struck the earth near him with a thunderous sound that vibrated the ground under Sonny's feet. The thought "My brain, my train" popped into Sonny's mind with a nudge from Raguel. In a moment of clarity, he knew that he could defeat the devil. Everything in his life had prepared him for this day. He wasn't here by accident; he had made this happen.

Sonny thought, *This is my day!*"

Instead of wondering what was going to happen, he thought to himself that something was going to happen with the forces of evil, and it was going to be okay. He was going to handle it and get through it. Alone in the woods and brimming with confidence, the four archangels appeared to him—Michael, Gabriel, Rafael, and Uriel. Their wings were fully extended and brilliantly glowing with different colors. Gabriel, the most terrifying of the four, smiled at Sonny; and they disappeared. They didn't say anything, but it was enough for Sonny. He knew he wasn't alone.

He left the forest and, throughout the day, said goodbye to his loved ones—his brother, Michael, and his sisters, Marcy and Yvette. He had lunch with his friend Brentavious, who was still working and in uniform. They ate at a coffee shop that the two would always go to, the Muffin Top. He went by his mother's house and told her how much he had always appreciated her strength and support. Finally he went to Holy Cross Church. It was early afternoon, and the parking lot was empty. It was a nice sunny afternoon in Los Angeles. There was a statue in front of the church of the Virgin Mary. Sonny walked over to the statue and kneeled. He had always had a profound connection with her, and he began to pray. He said the four prayers that he had always said before going to sleep every night of his life—the Our

Father, Hail Mary, Apostles' Creed, and Act of Contrition. Then he thanked God for all of the blessings in his life.

Sure, Sonny had a difficult and trying life, but he was also blessed. For all of the hurdles and mountains he had to go over, there was always an angel there to help him up. He asked for God to look out for his sons, family, and loved ones and apologized for his sins. Sonny felt a hand on his shoulder, and he looked up to see the angel Johel. Johel told Sonny he was proud of him and asked if he was ready for his toughest test.

Sonny asked, "My final test?"

Johel replied, "No, not the final test. For you, there is a tomorrow."

Sonny asked, "When?"

Like an angel with a pager, Johel told Sonny, "Any minute now, but let's just sit and talk until I got the word."

The two spoke like old friends about life, heaven, and the meaning of it all.

It was almost 3:00 p.m. in LA.

Johel told Sonny, "Okay, it is time for your spiritual call for service."

Sonny replied, "Go ahead. Dispatch."

Johel's wings appeared and wrapped around the two. They burst into light and constricted like fission bombs until they were transformed into two glowing spheres of light. They hovered about four feet above the ground and pulsed like a heartbeat for a second and then disappeared. They reappeared in an instant in Rome, Italy. Johel and Sonny were standing under the main bay of the Arch of Constantine, which is located about twenty-five yards from the Roman Colosseum. It was dark and almost midnight in Rome. Sonny asked Johel what time it was.

Johel replied, "Time for you to fulfill your destiny."

Sonny asked Johel what he meant. Johel told Sonny that the demons Azazel and Lilith were in the Colosseum and they weren't alone. Sonny asked who was with them. Johel said they had the child that he protected in New Brunswick a couple of years ago, the descendant of Miriam, Moses's sister. Sonny asked what would happen if he didn't go in there and just went home to see his forty-third birthday tomorrow. Johel told Sonny that they most certainly would kill the child, and then they would still have nine hours to kill Sonny if he went back to Los Angeles.

Sonny said aloud, "A real win-win, huh?" Sonny asked Johel if he was going in with him.

Johel told Sonny that this was his mandate that he agreed to. "Protect the descendants of light as Joshua did centuries ago."

Sonny said, "So save the girl, kill the demons, and live to see tomorrow. No problem."

Johel drew the staff of Moses from his back pocket and looked at it with awe and trepidation.

Johel told Sonny, "Your will is your weapon," and Johel disappeared.

Sonny looked at the staff, and it exploded into its full length. Sonny peered at the Roman Colosseum as the thoughts raced inside his head. He had been prepared for this moment his entire life. The angel Johel was gone, but that was okay. The atmosphere in the area started to reflect the storm of energy that Sonny was feeling. Sonny began to walk across the courtyard with his adrenaline surging and staff in hand. As he did so, thundering clouds, lighting, and thunder darkened the sky behind him. There was chain-link fencing blocking the entryway to the interior arena and archways spanning the circumference of the amphitheater. From Constantine's Arch, his attention was drawn to the left side of the Colosseum where three tiers of the building became four. There was a large copper-colored door and definitely fit the medieval facade.

As Sonny approached the magnificent structure, a violent storm raged above the Colosseum. Sonny tilted the staff toward the man-made chain-link fence and envisioned the fence melting in front of him, and it was so. It appeared that the staff not only responded to Sonny's will but to his emotion as well. Sonny was going to go through the copper door but noticed that there was an arch to his left that led to a first-floor tunnel. Sonny went into the tunnel, and it was dark and quiet except for the glow of his staff. Sonny was more at peace now and accepted that this was going to happen and it was okay.

He began to make his way through the tunnel around the left side of the arena above the lower-level labyrinth called the hypogeum. There were large interior arches to his right and man-made fencing to his left. The tunnel eventually opened up to the outside, and there was a large gateway to his right. The gateway opened into a large hallway with giant arches and an open area on the other side. It was dark, but the tunnel appeared to be about 150 feet. Iron gates stood open at the entrance, and there were passages to either side that were blocked structurally. This was the traditional entrance of the emperor. Sonny wasn't sure what awaited on the other side, but he started down the tunnel, the staff's ambient light revealing shapes and distance remaining as he walked.

As he entered what used to be the ground floor of the arena, the reality of the situation was electric. Lightning storms and clouds thundered overhead of the Colosseum. Constructed of red brick, concrete, and limestone, the Colosseum was a vortex for celestial energy. There was a reason that this place was chosen by the watchers for the conclusion of the seventieth son of the seventieth son prophecy. It would magnify their power. But it would also empower Sonny even more.

Only about one-quarter of the arena was covered with a platform. The point of entry was shaped in a semicircle and was about thirty feet in depth toward the middle of the arena. At the end of the platform, there was a small barrier wall that sat atop the lower level known as the hypogeum. There was a narrow walkway that stretched the length of the arena to the other side. It had been constructed in the modern area for tourists to observe the amphitheater. Straight ahead, he could see what looked like a four-post church altar, about thirty feet in front of him, at the end of the platform. It was stonelike, basic, and about four feet high by about four feet wide.

Lilith was sitting on the right side of the altar from Sonny's perspective. She was swinging her feet and laughing like a child. To her right, on the tabletop of the altar, was what looked like a four—to five-year-old girl in a white baptism gown. The child appeared to be unconscious but alive. To his left, he could see some man-made stadium seating, the kind you would expect to see at a high school baseball stadium, with a small decaying building next to that (probably used for gladiator staging at one time). To Sonny's right, he could see a couple of small structures like the one next to the stadium seating to his right. There were also a couple of tunnel entrances that led to an outer walkway around the arena.

On either side of the altar, spread apart on the platform, were two Nephilim, giant creatures that were the spawn of a watcher and a human woman. They were supposed to be put down by the archangels Gabriel and Michael centuries ago, but some survived. They resided in hell feeding on the souls of the condemned. Sonny recognized them from a dream he had a long time ago where he rescued Luke and Joshua in hell. With their appearance like that of a giant gargoyle, the sight of them would terrify anyone. But Sonny had seen them before and was indifferent to their intimidation.

What were they waiting for? It was almost midnight in Rome. Their time was almost up. Sonny walked toward the altar. As he did so, he saw the shadow of a man walking toward the altar from the other side on the narrow walkway from across the arena. Sonny couldn't make out much of the details of the figure except for glowing red eyes. Sonny reached the altar first and saw that there was what looked like an ancient Roman spearhead on the table. The shaft or staff portion of the spear had been broken, but about twelve inches remained. The spear blade was about fourteen inches in length. It was placed between Lilith and the child.

Sonny told Lilith, "Well, what's on our itinerary tonight?"

Lilith reached toward her mouth with her fist clenched, except for her index finger that extended over her lips, and said, "Shh."

Lilith was dark and sinister, and she oozed evil.

The male walking on the narrow walkway reached the altar, and it was no surprise that it was Azazel. He had taken many forms in Sonny's lifetime, but this was the form he had appeared as when he killed Sonny at five years old. Azazel was arrogant and evil and mission driven, with any sense of the angel he once was long gone.

Azazel told Sonny, "Hey, just a few minutes left, and it's your big day," as he looked up and around at the lightning and violent clouds and thunder overhead.

Sonny told Azazel to let the child go.

Azazel replied, "Sure. Just take a bite out of the spear of Longinus, and the world gets to keep spinning the way it is."

Azazel told Sonny that the watchers could kill him tonight and one more chip in the road to Revelations would be underway, but it would be so much easier if he just did it himself.

Sonny asked, "What's the deal with the spear?"

Azazel replied, "Why not? We have a couple of minutes."

Azazel explained that the spear of Longinus was also called the Spear of Destiny and it was the blade that pierced the side of Jesus during the crucifixion and it held a certain sentimental value to Azazel. Of course, Azazel was not telling the whole truth, and Sonny knew it.

Sonny said, "And?"

Azazel replied, "And it's one of the only objects that can totally eradicate one of you descendants of light. There's no coming back if the spear is used."

The two Nephilim began to close the distance between Sonny and the altar where the conversation was taking place.

Sonny noticed it and asked Azazel, "So how do you want this to go?"

Azazel replied, "Easy. We trade. You take the spear and give me the staff. Then you bury the spear in your stomach."

Sonny asked Azazel if he would let the child go if he did it.

Azazel said, "Of course, but let me give you a little more incentive."

Azazel looked past Sonny, toward the tunnels near the point of entry to the platform. He snapped his fingers, and two people emerged from a tunnel and started walking toward them. Again it was dark, but there was enough ambient light with the storms and the glow of the staff of Moses to make out that it was Simone and his ex-wife's divorce lawyer, a.k.a. Samjaya. Simone was a tall woman, but Samjaya still towered over her. Simone was on her trip to Egypt, and Sonny thought she was safe and out of the way.

Azazel told Sonny, "Turns out Cairo is pretty close to Rome."

Sonny was a cop. He'd been in enough hostage situations to know that, when the bad guy is showing enough of his head, you can take a headshot; but Sonny didn't have a gun. He did, however, have the staff of Moses and knew that it responded to his will.

Sonny surveyed the situation. Lilith was laughing at the makeshift altar. The DOL child was unconscious and in danger. There were two giant gargoyles growling and snarling at him. Azazel, Lucifer's lieutenant, was grinning and giving villain exposition as Sonny was in a temporary feedback loop in his head. Oh yeah, the woman whom he loved and who carried him out of a dark tunnel was a hostage behind him by the cursed watcher. The challenges of his life flashed in his mind—his death at five, Azazel reaching into his chest and squeezing his heart; the stabbing that came one inch of his aorta; and his wife walking out on him. But each time, he survived.

He started to have more positive memory flashes—the river of positive energy to heaven in his dream, the battle with Turiel and Zaqiel in New Brunswick, and the memory of his first kiss with Simone. It was like the five-minute anchor that he used to teach his karate students was playing out in his mind. As he kissed Simone in his mind and she looked up at him and smiled, he awoke from his temporary daydream. His head and his mind arose as his eyes fixated on Azazel's.

Sonny told Azazel, "No."

Azazel replied, "No what?"

Sonny told Azazel, "No to all of it."

Sonny's adrenaline raged within him like the storm that raged overhead. He held up the staff, and lightning struck down at him and entered the staff with a sharp, intense sound. Without any gap in time or hesitation, Sonny turned and redirected the staff at Samjaya. A bolt of lightning flew from the tip of the staff and struck Samjaya in the head. His head snapped around and stopped facing the wrong way on his shoulders. Like unplugging the cord on a vacuum cleaner, Samjaya's body went lifeless as he fell to the ground. Simone took a couple of steps back and was in shock.

She wasn't the only one. Lilith's cocky laugh disappeared and, she pissed herself a little. But there were still some bad-guy pieces on the chessboard. The Nephilim on Sonny's right began to charge at him. Sonny aimed the staff to the ground at the Nephilim's feet and began to rise it up slowly. As he did this, energy formed under the Nephilim. The monster rose in the air and flew over Sonny as Sonny directed it over his own head. The Nephilim crashed into the other Nephilim that was on Sonny's left in a violent collision. The two Nephilim tumbled into the man-made metal stadium seating that was on the left side of the platform. The two Nephilim began killing each other in a grotesque display, pulling each other's limbs apart in an uncontrolled display of violence. Sonny, Azazel, Lilith, and Simone watched for a couple of seconds until the Nephilim both took their last breaths. There was a brief silence.

Then Azazel said aloud, "Well, there's something you don't see every day."

Sonny looked at Lilith and directed the tip of his staff at her. They looked at each other without speaking for a moment, and then she turned to Azazel. She put her hands up in a nonverbal display of uncertainty, turned her palms up, and smiled.

Azazel said, "You bitch," as Lilith disappeared, fleeing from the battle.

Azazel picked up the spear by the broken dowel that used to be the shaft of the spear and held it to the throat of the girl that was out cold.

He waved his hand above her and said, "Awake."

The girl opened her eyes and screamed instantly. Then Azazel said, "Shh," and she stopped screaming. Azazel told Sonny kudos for taking some pieces off the board, but he still had checkmated. Azazel, the watcher demon that was collected and cool normally, was agitated and speaking very loudly. He demanded that Sonny give him the staff, or he would cut the girl's throat.

Sonny told Azazel that he would comply. He raised his hands and said, "Okay, okay."

Azazel was pissed. He exclaimed, "Now, asshole! The clock is ticking!"

Simone had walked closer as the two were talking and yelled for Sonny not to do it.

Azazel waved his free hand and said, "Shut up."

Simone fell to the ground and was asleep.

Azazel screamed, "The staff, now!"

Sonny released his grip on the staff as it was being held in his right hand. The staff floated vertically for a moment as Azazel stepped around the altar and was excited, believing that he had won by taking away Sonny's weapon. Sonny's right hand was open but sideways like in a handshake position. Sonny rotated his hand to palm up, and the staff floated toward Azazel, who was standing about three to five feet away at this point. Azazel grabbed the staff from the air with his left hand and looked at it in awe for a second.

He said aloud, "Only an angel can bequeath the staff, so no demon has ever held it."

Sonny took a step toward Azazel, and Azazel awoke from his temporary distraction.

He said, "Not so fast," as he directed the tip of the staff toward the small girl who was unconscious again, threatening the child with the use of the celestial weapon. Azazel told Sonny, "Don't forget the best part. Bury this blade in your stomach."

Azazel turned the blade of the spear around toward himself, displaying the shaft, and extended his arm toward Sonny to hand him the blade. Sonny took the blade as Azazel shouted for Sonny to kill himself or else. By this point, Azazel had a firm grip on the staff with both hands. Sonny had the Spear of Destiny in his right hand by the shaft with the blade extending backward, toward his forearm, not exactly in the optimal suicide-stabbing position. Sonny reached toward Azazel with his left hand, and the staff of Moses lunged quickly back to Sonny, taking Azazel with it. Azazel involuntarily moved toward Sonny with his arms extended and staff in his hands. Sonny grasped the middle of the staff split between Azazel's grip. Sonny buried the spear in Azazel's chest with his right hand so deep the point of the spear protruded through Azazel's back. Azazel was in shock as his body started to evaporate from his feet toward his head like sand sifting through someone's hands. Azazel was a powerful demon. Throughout his existence, he'd been stabbed, shot, and even blown up; and he had survived. Also, a blade used for evil couldn't be used against evil. Azazel disintegrated into nothing as Sonny stared into his eyes until he had no eyes left.

Simone and the small girl awoke, disoriented but alive. Sonny told the girl that she was okay as Simone stood and walked to Sonny quickly, and the two embraced. Sonny looked down at his watch and saw that it was just after midnight. He had made it. All three looked up at the sky because the thunder, lightning, and violent storms had subsided when Azazel was killed, and peace fell upon Sonny's mind. A golden light in the sky was descending down toward them. As it drew closer, they could see that the figure was humanlike, with giant wings extending out like breaks to slow his descent. The angel Johel flapped his glowing white wings as he came to a stop onto the platform. This was the first time that Simone and the little girl had ever seen an angel and stood motionless and speechless as he landed.

Johel took a couple of steps toward Sonny, his pride for him beaming in his expression. Johel asked Sonny how he knew the blade would kill Azazel. Sonny told Johel that he had been studying methods to kill demons since he was five years old, and the Spear of Destiny was one of them. Johel said that Azazel believed the spear was an evil tool used to do an evil thing.

Sonny told Johel, "Yes, but after it pierced the side of Christ, the unknown Roman soldier famously said, 'Surely this man was the Son of God.' That unknown soldier was given the name Longinus. Longinus was, in essence, the first Christian and walked away from his station to follow Christ. The spear became a holy weapon after that."

Johel asked Sonny how he knew the staff of Moses could not be wielded by Azazel.

Sonny explained that the staff only obeyed him and that it was tied to his will and his emotions. "My brain, my train."

Johel called the girl to him and said he would take her home. Johel put his arm around the little girl, and his wing followed.

Sonny handed Johel the Spear of Destiny and started to hand him the staff of Moses as well. Johel told Sonny to keep the staff. Johel told Sonny that they won this battle, but the war was not over. Johel asked Sonny if he wanted a ride back to LA after he took the girl home.

Simone looked up at Sonny and said, "Do you want to get a room in Rome for the night or fight demons in LA for eight more hours?"

Sonny looked back at the angel Johel and said, "I think we'll catch a plane home later."

Johel smiled as his wings constricted around him and the little girl, and they transformed into two spheres of light that pulsed like a heartbeat for a moment and then disappeared.

THE END

There are thousands of people that suffer from anxiety, PTSD, or depression. Everyone carries a cross or a burden in their minds that only they know about. For some, the weight is like a heavy coat; for others, the weight is like that of a piano. This book was written to tell an entertaining story and make a profit doing it—yes, that's true—but also to let people know that they are not alone. It's about faith and willpower and hopefully to inspire people to understand that their thoughts and will determine their realities. We create our own demons most of the time, and we are the only ones who can slay them. It is not my wish for notoriety. I hope everyone who reads this book can find something that resonates with them that leads to peace of mind and hope in their hearts. What we focus on, what we value, and the lives we lead are within our control. Breath and live in the moment.

You can slay your demons.

AMEN.

ABOUT THE AUTHOR

Audie Ward was raised by a great mom in Upstate New York. When he was five years old (before there was the term SIDS death), he died. He was brought back thanks to a neighbor who happened to be a doctor and provided CPR. He's a retired police sergeant after almost a twenty-four-year career. He was very nearly murdered in the line of duty. He has two fantastic sons whom he loves, and they anchor him every day. He has done a lot in life, and he experienced anxiety. The author painted the yin-yang lions on the cover of this book to represent balance in life.